Praise for *No One Will Hire Me!*

"UNUSUALLY HELPFUL AND MODESTLY PRICED . . . the print equivalent of a process and resource-rich workshop." – **Joyce Lain Kennedy, Syndicated Career Columnist, Tribune Media Services**

"APPROPRIATE FOR ANYONE FACING A JOB OR CAREER TRANSITION**, from ex-offenders to students to transitioning military to dislocated workers. An affordable addition to any Resource Room." – *NAWDP Advantage,* **National Association of Workforce Development Professionals**

"A SOLIDLY WRITTEN AND EXTREMELY PRACTICAL guide designed especially for intelligent job-seekers who have trouble getting hired because they do not fully understand business culture protocols. An extensive, easy-to-follow, and straightforward information manual on identifying and avoiding mistakes as well as what positive attitudes to project. *No One Will Hire Me!* warns against such commonplace errors as spending too much time on the Internet and not enough time networking when searching for a job, arriving late in the interview waiting lobby when other personnel may be watching, failing to thank the interviewer for his time, and a great deal more. Highly recommended for serious applicants entering the job market for the first time, as well as those who because of corporate downsizing must re-enter the competitive job application process. *No One Will Hire Me!* is a 'must-read' for anyone having to adapt to the conditions of today's job market." – **Midwest Book Review**

By Ron and Caryl Krannich

CAREER AND BUSINESS BOOKS

101 Secrets of Highly Effective Speakers
201 Dynamite Job Search Letters
The $100,000+ Entrepreneur
America's Top 100 Jobs for People Without a Four-Year Degree
America's Top Jobs for People Re-Entering the Workforce
America's Top Internet Job Sites
Best Jobs for the 21st Century
Best Resumes and Letters for Ex-Offenders
Blue Collar Resume and Job Hunting Guide
Change Your Job, Change Your Life
The Complete Guide to Public Employment
The Directory of Federal Jobs and Employers
Discover the Best Jobs for You!
Dynamite Salary Negotiations
Dynamite Tele-Search
The Educator's Guide to Alternative Jobs and Careers
The Ex-Offender's Job Hunting Guide
The Ex-Offender's Quick Job Hunting Guide
Find a Federal Job Fast!
From Air Force Blue to Corporate Gray
From Army Green to Corporate Gray
From Navy Blue to Corporate Gray
Get a Raise in 7 Days
High Impact Resumes and Letters
I Can't Believe They Asked Me That!
I Want to Do Something Else, But I'm Not Sure What It Is
Interview for Success
The Job Hunting Guide: Transitioning From College to Career
Job Hunting Tips for People With Hot and Not-So-Hot Backgrounds
Job Interview Tips for People With Not-So-Hot Backgrounds
Jobs and Careers With Nonprofit Organizations
Military Transition to Civilian Success
Military Resumes and Cover Letters
Nail the Cover Letter!
Nail the Job Interview!
Nail the Resume!
No One Will Hire Me!
Overcoming Barriers to Employment
Overcoming 101 More Barriers to Employment
Re-Careering in Turbulent Times
Savvy Interviewing
The Savvy Networker
The Savvy Resume Writer
Win the Interview, Win the Job

TRAVEL AND INTERNATIONAL BOOKS

Best Resumes and CVs for International Jobs
The Complete Guide to International Jobs and Careers
The Directory of Websites for International Jobs
International Jobs Directory
Jobs for Travel Lovers
Shopping in Exotic Places
Shopping the Exotic South Pacific
Travel Planning On the Internet
Treasures and Pleasures of Australia
Treasures and Pleasures of Bermuda
Treasures and Pleasures of China
Treasures and Pleasures of Egypt
Treasures and Pleasures of Hong Kong
Treasures and Pleasures of India
Treasures and Pleasures of Indonesia
Treasures and Pleasures of Italy
Treasures and Pleasures of Mexico
Treasures and Pleasures of Paris
Treasures and Pleasures of Rio and São Paulo
Treasures and Pleasures of Santa Fe, Taos, and Albuquerque
Treasures and Pleasures of Singapore
Treasures and Pleasures of South America
Treasures and Pleasures of Southern Africa
Treasures and Pleasures of Thailand and Myanmar
Treasures and Pleasures of Turkey
Treasures and Pleasures of Vietnam and Cambodia

No One
Will Hire Me!
3rd Edition

Avoid 17 Mistakes and Win the Job

Ron and Caryl Krannich, Ph.Ds

IMPACT PUBLICATIONS
Manassas Park, VA

No One Will Hire Me!

Third Edition

ISBN: 971-1-57023-266-6 (13-digit); 1-57023-266-0 (10-digit)

Library of Congress: 2006935162

Publisher: For information on Impact Publications, including current and forthcoming publications, authors, press kits, online bookstore, and submission requirements, visit the left navigation bar on the front page of our main company website: www.impactpublications.com.

Publicity/Rights: For information on publicity, author interviews, and subsidiary rights, contact the Media Relations Department: Tel. 703-361-7300, Fax 703-335-9486, or email: query@impactpublications.com.

Sales/Distribution: All bookstore sales are handled through Impact's trade distributor: National Book Network, 15200 NBN Way, Blue Ridge Summit, PA 17214, Tel. 1-800-462-6420. All special sales and distribution inquiries should be directed to the publisher: Sales Department, IMPACT PUBLICATIONS, 9104 Manassas Drive, Suite N, Manassas Park, VA 20111-5211, Tel. 703-361-7300, Fax 703-335-9486, or email: query@impactpublications.com.

Contents

1

Mother Was Both Right and Wrong!

W E'VE OFTEN HEARD the laments of the frustrated job seeker – *"No one will hire me!"* or *"There are no jobs available!"* Such individuals spend weeks looking for a job, experiencing many rejections, and complaining about life without a job. Nothing much positive happens as they gradually lose their self-esteem and become depressed at the whole thought of continuing their seemingly fruitless job search. Desperate to get a job, they often take the first one they can find regardless of whether or not it's a good fit for their interests and skills.

The Problem May Be Close At Hand

While the *"No one will hire me!"* plaint implies the general lack of jobs available for the job seeker in what may be a tough job market, on closer examination we find the story is much more complex. The problem may be nearer to home and relatively easy to solve. In fact, a little "how to" knowledge on job search realities may go a long way to getting hired.

This so-called hiring problem comes as no surprise to career professionals who know this scenario all too well. Just ask the frustrated job seeker a few basic questions, such as *"What exactly do you want to do?,"* *"What kind of resume did you write?,"* or *"How many new contacts did you make this week?"* and the answers often reveal more fundamental problems in how the individual organizes and implements a job search. Indeed, we frequently find the problem centers on specific **attitudes and behaviors** of the job seeker who makes several key mistakes that prevent him from achieving job search success. These attitudes and behaviors need to change. As we will quickly see, job seekers with the right combination of attitudes and behaviors have a **behavioral advantage** over other candidates in today's highly competitive job market. Your goal should be to quickly present a decisive behavioral advantage over others.

For Smart People Who Fail

Understanding these mistakes and taking corrective actions to achieve job search success is the subject of this book. It's written for anyone – from those first entering the job market to experienced professionals experiencing job loss or making a career change – who needs to better organize or jump-start their job search. This is not a "blame the victim" book about people who make stupid or dumb mistakes, nor one designed for someone with serious psychological problems or disabilities requiring therapy or some form of specialized professional intervention. Rather, it's about why smart people frequently fail in finding a job, as well as why these same people are often less than successful in finding a really good job – one they do well and enjoy doing. Some reasons are cultural in nature – for example, wise advice your mother gave you as a child but which may work against you when you grow up. Other reasons relate to social interaction and communication skills, from writing a resume and letter to handling face-to-face networking and job interviews. And still other reasons relate to the lack of understanding how a unique process actually works in reality – mistakes that can be corrected by learning new behaviors and/or acquiring new habits of success. Job seekers often make stupid mistakes, like showing up for an interview 15 minutes late, but most mistakes tend to relate to culture and an inadequate understanding of the job search

> *Most mistakes tend to relate to culture and an inadequate understanding of the job search process.*

process. These mistakes can be quickly corrected with a little "how to" knowledge.

Learn From Mistakes Other People Make

We're really not sure how people learn and then go on to change their behaviors. Sometimes it may be life-changing events, such as being fired or arrested, having children, going bankrupt, receiving a prestigious award, facing a serious illness, experiencing a death in the family, or contemplating the events surrounding "9/11" – special failures, successes, or shocking events that can alter our values and behaviors. In other cases it may be special words or deeds of mentors or a renewed sense of purpose and responsibility stimulated by new goals and attitudes.

Whatever the case, we do know that people can learn from their **successes**. Indeed, career counselors often advise job seekers to identify their achievements – the key building blocks for effective resumes, letters, and interviews – by analyzing their successes.

You may learn more from understanding mistakes than from analyzing successes.

At the same time, we can learn from our **mistakes** if we have a clear understanding of what went wrong and how to take corrective action. In fact, you may learn more from understanding mistakes than from analyzing successes. But how does such learning modify behavior? It could have unintended consequences. To just understand what went wrong may have a negative effect on some individuals if the individual decides to withdraw, minimizes future risks, and abandons what were once important dreams and goals.

Our task here is to get a better understanding of mistakes job seekers make and provide sound advice on how to take positive actions that lead to renewed success.

What Mother Said Was Often Right

Caring mothers counsel their children in many different and positive ways. While your mother's words may not have rung true for you early in life, they often have a way of coming back in later years as "words of wisdom." Let's call these "Mom's 10 Basic Rules for Success":

1. Get a good education.
2. Find a good job.
3. Work hard.
4. Save your money.
5. Associate with the right people.
6. Treat others nicely.
7. Be cooperative and help out.
8. Watch your time.
9. Be honest and charitable.
10. Marry well.

Taking these rules together, mother seemed to know a lot about getting ahead in life, especially if you concentrated on her first five rules!

Then Sometimes Mother Was Wrong

But mother doesn't always know best for success later in life. She also may have been very protective of you in your youth. She wanted you to be safe, likable, and perhaps sweet and shy. Mothers often teach their children these three cautionary communication rules:

1. **Don't talk to strangers** – they could take advantage of you or harm you; watch out for predators.

2. **Don't discuss money with others** – it's not anyone's business what you or they make.

3. **Don't talk about yourself** – no one likes boastful or egocentric people who brag about themselves.

If you are like many other job seekers, you probably recognize all three rules as ways you still orient yourself to others. You probably don't like making cold calls as part of a networking campaign, you feel uncomfortable talking about money, and you have difficulty tooting your horn to others – all important communication skills for conducting an effective job search. You may even teach these same rules to your own children who, in turn, will pass them on to their children. Not surprisingly, these rules are part of our communication culture. They are associated with reticence, caution, and untrustworthiness in many relationships, especially when dealing with strangers.

While these rules may have served you well as you were growing up, they actually may work against you as an adult. Indeed, these three deeply ingrained cultural rules often prevent adults from taking positive actions that could enhance their careers. Especially when people are conducting a job search, these rules have a negative impact on developing four key job search skills:

Important job search skills	Mother's negative rules
■ Networking	Don't talk to strangers
■ Writing resumes and letters	Don't brag about yourself
■ Interviewing	Don't talk about yourself
■ Negotiating salary	Don't talk about money

If you were raised in such a cultural environment, you may face some serious communication challenges inherited from your mother! For example, if you are reluctant to talk to strangers, how in the world will you ever be able to develop and implement an effective networking campaign, which is key to uncovering job leads and gaining invaluable advice about job opportunities? Maybe your networking activities follow Mom's more successful "associate with the right people" rule, but somewhere along the way you'll need to make cold calls to strangers in order to expand your network. Many people also hate making cold calls. It's because they have to talk to strangers!

How can you communicate your qualifications on resumes, in letters, and during job interviews if you can't clearly articulate what you do well and enjoy doing, with special emphasis on enumerating your achievements? If you haven't learned to talk naturally about promoting yourself to others in a positive and purposeful way, or if you are shy about yourself, then you won't be able to put your best foot forward to strangers who need to know what it is you will do for them based upon their knowledge of your past pattern of achievements.

And how will you negotiate a fair compensation package if you don't know what others are making because you won't talk about money to other people? If you are like many other job seekers, you may accept the first offer you receive because you are basically "salary dumb." On the other hand, smart job seekers know exactly what they are worth because they have learned to talk about money with the right people.

Thank your mother for the first 10 rules for success. But remember the next three rules were meant to both safeguard and socialize children. Now that you've grown up, it's time to start conversing with strangers, asking questions about money, and talking about yourself to others. These actions constitute important rules for achieving job search success. We will return to these rules in subsequent chapters when we examine several key mistakes job seekers make.

> *Thank your mother for the first 10 rules but not for the last three, which are to safeguard and socialize children.*

A Rogue's Gallery of Bad Habits

Most people act based upon well-defined **patterns of behavior**. If you analyze your patterns, you'll be able to get a better understanding of what, why, and how you do things, including how you get and keep a job. Some people, for example, engage in addictive and abusive behaviors, from drugs and alcohol to eating and the Internet. Their lives are often out of control and unpredictable. Many people lack career goals or they can't explain what they want to do. Lacking purpose, they have difficulty focusing and thus appear aimless and in need of direction. Other people hang around the wrong crowds and thereby lack decent connections for networking their way into a good job. And still other people talk too much, make spelling and grammatical errors, show up late for interviews, dress inappropriately, give bad answers to interview questions, appear disingenuous, and ask the wrong questions of employers. Once on the job they may lack focus, attention to detail, trustworthiness, and an ability to work well with others. Many of these behaviors become bad habits that work against people in both the job market and workplace. No one wants to hire people exhibiting such detrimental workplace behaviors.

Seeking Different Levels of Help

The fact that you are reading this book may say something about the level of help you need or seek. At a very basic level, you may just be in need of a little knowledge that can make a difference in how to conduct your job search. If this is the case, you should find the book useful in fine-tuning your job search. It will appeal to your rational self.

You'll learn about several mistakes job seekers make because they lack an understanding of how the job search process works in practice. These mistakes can easily be overcome by making adjustments in the way you approach the job market and employers. You'll learn, for example, that you may be wasting time responding to classified ads and posting resumes online. We'll advise you to fine-tune your job search by spending more time on networking for information, advice, and referrals for uncovering job leads and getting job interviews. This may the most important mistake you make and the most critical corrective action you need to take in order to re-energize your job search. In other words, a little new knowledge may go a long way for you as you

> *Some people need a structure, an interactive process, and motivation to successfully get through the job search process.*

decide to change your approach to reality. As a self-starter, you are off and running on your own as you test your new knowledge for achieving greater success. You are our ideal user – someone who can read, understand, and successfully apply this book to your life.

At another level, you may understand all the mistakes you make, but you need something more than just understanding and a book to get you started and sustained in the right direction. You need a structure, an interactive process, and motivation to successfully get through the job search process. Here, you may want to contract for the services of a career professional who can help you at various stages of your job search. Career professionals wear many different hats and offer many different services, skill sets, and levels of structure – from resume writers and career coaches to career managers, certified career counselors, and psychologists. Their services are inexpensive to costly, depending on whom you contract with for what types of services. If available through local government, community colleges, or special community centers, some of these services may be free to local residents. Many of the services involve testing and assessment, organizing a job search campaign, and developing specific job search skills, such as networking, resume and letter writing, interviewing, and negotiating salary. Individuals who need this level of help are not self-starters who can just pick up a how-to book and run with it. They may be good at understanding a process, but when it comes to implementation, they need someone beside them to help them through various steps in the process. Their success depends in large part on a structure that will keep them focused and motivated throughout the process. As such, they need a professional to help them apply their new-found job search knowledge.

At a third level, many individuals may be dealing with some fundamental learning and behavioral problems that need to be addressed with the assistance of trained specialists and psychologists who are experienced in handling everything from learning disabilities and addictions to mental illness. These are not subjects for career counselors who lack training and certification in handling such challenging issues. In these cases, therapy or prescription drugs may be the best approach to getting one's life back on track or at least under some type of control. Take, for example, individuals who have difficulty concentrating on their work or keeping a job for more than six months. Some of these individuals may have Attention Deficit and Hyperactivity Disorders (ADHD). Individuals who constantly come to work late and have difficulty doing their work may show signs of more fundamental behavioral problems, from bad work habits and drug abuse to mental health issues, such as depression or bipolar disorder – problems that increasingly affect the workplace and are frequent subjects of employee assistance (counseling) programs.

The problems are obviously more serious for an individual who has difficulty finding a job after a year has passed. In a recent case, while writing this book, we encountered someone who had read all the job search books but still couldn't land a decent job after nearly four years. She was paranoid, feeling everyone was discriminating against her because of her age – 55. Then she became a menacing personality by threatening employers with legal action. To further jade her personality, her college advisor gave her this "wise" but revealing advice – sell Cadillacs – even though you're getting your master's degree in technology! What no one had the heart to tell her was that she probably had a serious personality disorder – the job seeker and employee from hell! Nobody wants a social loser or one with difficult mental baggage. She was the perfect candidate for a therapist who might be able to help change her attitudes, personality, and behavior through cognitive behavioral therapy. But a book or a career counselor would probably further frustrate her as well as exacerbate her already self-destructive personality. This was literally a case where no one wanted to hire her – and for good reasons!

If any of these examples in our third case represent your situation, this book may do little for you other than help you recognize the fact that you need to seek the right type of professional assistance rather than continue in denial. We'll readdress this issue of seeking out different levels of professional advice and assistance in Chapter 17.

A Sequence of Multiple Job Search Errors

Whether you can best benefit from a book, career counselor, or a therapist is something you need to decide based upon an analysis of your situation. What we outline in the following pages are some of the basic realities of the job search process along with corresponding mistakes and suggested corrective actions. Over the years we have seen these mistakes recur over and over again. They've become even more apparent as much of the job search has moved to the Internet. Taken together, these mistakes form a pattern of errors that contributes to job search failure for individuals who should have a better understanding of marketing themselves to potential employers. In most cases, these are unfortunate errors because they could be corrected with a little bit of knowledge about the realities of conducting an effective job search.

Our experience is that many job seekers make serious to awful job search mistakes throughout the job search, from developing an initial job search plan to negotiating the final job offer. Most of the errors are made in reference to this sequential 10-step job search process, which we further elaborate in Chapter 4:

Sequential Activities	Type of Stage
1. Develop positive attitudes	Motivation
2. Seek assistance	Outreach
3. Select a useful approach	Investigative
4. Identify skills and abilities	Investigative
5. Specify goals	Investigative
6. Conduct research	Investigative
7. Write resumes and letters	Writing
8. Network	Employer contact
9. Interview	Employer contact
10. Negotiate salary	Employer contact

The first seven stages can be done on your own with little or no interaction with others. Indeed, you can complete most of these activities in the privacy of your home or office using books, tests, exercises, and the Internet. The final three activities involve interaction with others, which means using important social and communication skills.

At each stage mistakes tend to multiply. For example, many job seekers make a combination of 45 mistakes just in reference to writing, producing, distributing, and following up resumes and letters (see Chapter 9). In the end, the 15 key mistakes we discuss in the remainder of this book may include over 200 specific errors job seekers make. A disproportionate number of these mistakes center on three critical job search steps – writing resumes, networking, and interviewing.

What's Your Mistake-Prone Job Search I.Q.?

Some job seekers are more prone to making mistakes than others. Respond to each of the following agree/disagree statements on a scale of 5 to 1 (strongly agree = 5; strongly disagree = 1) in order to identify how prone you may be to making job search mistakes:

1. I can identify my strongest abilities and skills.   5 4 3 2 1

2. I know what I like and dislike in work.   5 4 3 2 1

3. I know what motivates me to excel at work.   5 4 3 2 1

4. I can list my seven top achievements and
   explain them to an employer.   5 4 3 2 1

5. I have a well-defined career objective that
   guides my job search from beginning to end.   5 4 3 2 1

6. I can clearly explain to employers what I
   do well and enjoy doing.   5 4 3 2 1

7. I can specify in 50 words or less why an
   employer should hire me.   5 4 3 2 1

8. I can write different types of effective
   resumes and job search letters.   5 4 3 2 1

9. I know whom to send my resume and
   letters to.   5 4 3 2 1

10. I know how to properly close a cover
    letter and follow up.   5 4 3 2 1

11. I can identify and target employers
    I want to interview.   5 4 3 2 1

12. I can develop a job referral network.   5 4 3 2 1

13. I know how to use the Internet to conduct
    employment research and network.   5 4 3 2 1

14. I know which websites are best for posting
    my resume and browsing job postings.   5 4 3 2 1

15. I know how much time I should spend
    conducting an online job search.   5 4 3 2 1

16. I can persuade employers to interview me.   5 4 3 2 1

17. I have a list of at least 10 employer-centered
    questions I need to ask during interviews.   5 4 3 2 1

18. I know the best time to talk about salary
    with an employer.   5 4 3 2 1

19. I have a clear idea of what I want to
    accomplish at work this coming week.   5 4 3 2 1

20. I set priorities and follow through on the
    most important tasks first.   5 4 3 2 1

21. I make minor decisions quickly.   5 4 3 2 1

22. I know how to say "no" and do so.   5 4 3 2 1

23. I know what I want to do with my life over
    the next 10 years.   5 4 3 2 1

24. I have a clear pattern of accomplishments
    which I can explain to employers with
    examples.   5 4 3 2 1

25. I usually stay with an employer for three or
    more years.   5 4 3 2 1

26. I have little difficulty in making cold calls
    and striking up conversations with strangers.   5 4 3 2 1

27. I always arrive at a job interview on time or
    with a few minutes to spare.   5 4 3 2 1

28. I immediately return most phone calls and
    respond to important emails and letters.   5 4 3 2 1

29. I control my time well rather than let other
    people control it.   5 4 3 2 1

30. I usually take responsibility for my own
    actions rather than blame other people for
    my situation or circumstances.   5 4 3 2 1

TOTAL J.S.I.Q. [   ]

If your total J.S.I.Q. (Job Search I.Q.) score is 135 or above, you are least likely to make the many mistakes outlined in this book. If your J.S.I.Q. is below 110, you can benefit a great deal from reading this book and putting it into practice. Upon completion of this book, your J.S.I.Q. should increase substantially!

But which statements you disagreed with may indicate how mistake-prone you may be in the future and how difficult or easy it will be for you to take corrective actions. If, for example, most of your "disagrees" were in response to the first 18 statements, taking corrective action may be relatively easy and most of the advice can be found within the pages of this book. The reason for this is that the first 18 statements relate to your **knowledge** in reference to conducting an effective job search. If you responded "disagree" to any of these statements, you can take corrective action by following "how to" advice or tips or learning new job search skills. However, if many of your "disagrees" were in response to the last 12 statements (19-30), you may be very mistake-prone; taking corrective action may be very difficult for you. The reason for this is that statements 19-30 relate to your **patterns of behavior**. Many of these behaviors deal with your attitudes, motivations, self-management practices, and social interactive skills. These patterns of behavior can be modified by changing your attitudes and orientations to people, things, and situations. They require breaking old habits that lead to recurring mistakes rather than just acquiring more knowledge. Change, in this case, takes place through acquiring more knowledge. Change, in this case, takes place through behavior modification rather than through understanding.

The following chapters identify numerous mistakes which can be corrected through a combination of knowledge and behavioral modification. The easiest mistakes to correct are knowledge-based ones. The real challenge will be in correcting mistakes that require modifying your behavior which, in turn, means changing your attitudes and motivations.

Resources for Getting Started

If you feel you can benefit from additional print resources as well as audios, videos, and software, we recommend visiting our online career bookstore, which includes hundreds of useful job and career resources, along with escapist travel resources:

www.impactpublications.com

You also may want to visit our career advice website for information on conducting an effective job search and getting ahead in the workplace:

www.winningthejob.com

We also publish several other books on various steps in the job search process, from skills assessment and goal setting (*I Want to Do Something Else, But I'm Not Sure What It Is*) to networking (*The Savvy Networker*), resume writing (*The Savvy Resume Writer*), interviewing (*Win the Interview, Win the Job*), and salary negotiations (*Dynamite Salary Negotiations*). Our *Change Your Job, Change Your Life* deals with the whole job search, and *America's Top Internet Job Sites* serves as a directory for effectively using the Internet. We also produce several books related to the military and ex-offenders. For more information on these and other related career resources, see the order form at the end of this book as well as visit Impact Publications's online bookstore.

Make No More Mistakes!

We wish you well as you navigate through today's challenging job market and seek a behavioral advantage over the competition. Always keep in mind that finding a job does not come easily, even for seemingly seasoned and successful professionals. For most serious candidates, job finding is hard but rewarding work if done properly.

So let's get started by addressing several mistakes job seekers make to see how they relate to your situation. Each of the remaining chapters outlines a key job search mistake as well as includes things you can do to take corrective action. We believe you can learn a lot about the job search – and yourself – by examining the mistakes other people make. Hopefully you will avoid these mistakes by acquiring new knowledge about the best way to conduct an effective job search.

If you have recurring behavior patterns that cause you to make these mistakes, or what we address as "career-limiting habits" in Chapter 18, it's time to come clean about such patterns or habits rather than remain in denial. Acknowledge the truth about yourself and make some fundamental changes in how you relate to other people. For in the end, the job search is an intense people activity – you interacting with others who can either help or hinder your job search and your future career development. Make sure your attitudes, motivations, and behaviors are worthy of your goals, the job you seek, and the life you want. For in the end, you are your own best self!

2

Abandon Dreams and Lack Goals

W E'VE ALL HAD IMPORTANT dreams about our future. Perhaps in childhood you dreamed of growing up and becoming a firefighter, policeman, teacher, or soldier. If you were on the high school basketball team, maybe you dreamed of someday becoming an NBA star. Perhaps you had a lead role in a school play and thought of becoming a star on Broadway. Or perhaps you're still dreaming today of the perfect job or lifestyle – becoming the CEO of a major corporation or the U.S. Secretary of State or traveling to exotic places around the world.

While some dreams come true, others become fantasies we abandon. Still others become motivators for setting and achieving goals.

The Art of Sailing Without a Rudder

Much of life approximates the art of sailing – you may have a destination in mind (your plan or goal), but many variables, which to different degrees are within your control, determine if and when you reach your charted destination. Your boat must be well equipped with such basics as

15

sails, navigation gear, and a good rudder, and you should be skilled at planning and handling what may become unpredictable winds and waves. Reaching your final destination will depend on how well you handle the many ingredients that go into a successful journey. While you may encounter some bad luck along the way, your skills at navigating through troubled waters should serve you well in reaching your final goal.

But what happens to your boat if you leave shore without a plan, a rudder, or basic navigation skills? You'll most likely have a very interesting, and hopefully lucky, journey along the way to nowhere in particular. If you are a good storyteller, you'll be able to share many anecdotes about different events in your rather spontaneous journey to somewhere.

From Go-Getter to Getter

Unfortunately, many people stop dreaming and setting goals after a few years of "real world" experience. This often comes at an early age – before their 30's and before they've had a chance to pass through life's many different seasons. Busy people buffeted by external forces that seem beyond their control, they become what we call "getters" rather than "go-getters" – they get an education; they get married and get a family; they get a house; they get a job; they get divorced; they get in debt; they get depressed; they get stressed; they get taxed; they get retired; they get sick; they get abandoned; and they get buried. Some even occasionally get lucky! Somewhere along life's bumpy highway their dreams and goals get ambushed by the many daily ups and downs of living that often center around family, finances, and jobs. Indeed, what they don't "get" is much control over their lives.

Long ago abandoning dreams that could have helped shape their future, many people learn to go with the flow of life. They often find living is tough and working is no fun. For some people, life frequently gets out of control; they have difficulty finding and keeping jobs; they get financially over their heads and deeply indebted; and some engage in addictive and self-destructive behaviors that beg for professional intervention. As they get older and abandon their personal goals to family responsibilities, their dreams often shift from themselves to their children – they hope the little ones will have a better future. Accordingly they socialize their children according to the "basic rules for success" as outlined on page 4 of Chapter 1.

Unfortunately, the two saddest mistakes job seekers make are to abandon their dreams and fail to articulate goals or a purpose. Without a vision of the future, people may find little meaning in the present. Like much of their life, they lack purpose, direction, and meaning. Like a ship without a rudder, they wander all over the sea of jobs. What, for example, do you want to do with the rest of your life? What is your life all about? Survival? Momentary pleasure? Happiness? As a result, such goal-less people often present a fuzzy picture to employers of someone who doesn't know what he or she wants to do other than get the job in question and make more money. Lacking clear goals and thus a driving passion to go

> *The two saddest mistakes job seekers make are to abandon their dreams and fail to articulate goals.*

along with their goals, these people do not appeal much to employers in search of purposeful and passionate individuals with employer- and career-centered goals.

Be Honest, But Not Stupid

Some people really impress us. In fact, we still remember vividly someone we interviewed for a job. While technically very well qualified for the job, in the middle of the interview she asked us a seemingly thoughtful job search question: *"Do you recommend putting an objective on a resume?"* She obviously didn't have one on her resume. And before she let us respond (unknown to her, we are big advocates of putting objectives on resumes!), she began lecturing us on the stupidity of objectives on resumes. She even became animated. Leaning forward and rubbing her index finger and thumb together, she said, *"This is what all job seekers really want – more money!"* She thought having a job objective on a resume was a dumb idea since it was obvious what everyone wanted when looking for a job. With that revealing little lecture about her goals and attitudes, we didn't need to spend more time with this candidate. We appreciated her honesty, which also verified her sole motivation and indicated a possible host of other potential problems we would likely inherit had we hired her. As an employer, we saw these relatively predictable patterns of behavior in this individual, which raised serious red flags about hiring her:

- **Lack of tact.** Being too frank translates as being naively blunt and stupid in the eyes of the employer.

- **Bad attitude.** We would get lots of attitude from this person, which we were certain we did not need in our workplace.

- **Brutal frankness with customers.** She would most likely use a customer service approach that would send customers running for the hills – lost business that would never return.

- **Talks too much.** Doesn't know when to quit talking and focus on what's important to her work. She would probably have diarrhea of the mouth at work.

- **Self-centered "me first" approach to the job – money, money, money.** We would have to constantly explain to her that this is a job which pays money for performance.

- **Difficult to fit sharp personality into the organization.** As she pollutes the office environment with her unsolicited attitudes and loose mouth, other employees would soon ask why did we hire **her**? For what?

She would predictably be the employee who would become more trouble than she was worth – constantly focusing on making more money with little evidence of performance or interest in the job or company. We have seen this pattern before, and her words were good predictors of many bad things to come for us and others in our company.

We took her question and lecture calmly – still amazed by what stupid things job seekers can say in job interviews – and thanked her for coming to the interview. After she left, we examined her resume more carefully. Indeed, she had no objective and no clear pattern of career development. She also revealed another clear behavioral pattern as evidenced in her chronology of jobs – she was a perennial job hopper, tap dancing from one job to another She normally stayed on a job about 18 months and then moved on to another. We sensed she was going nowhere with her career, except to another short-term job, where she might be more trouble than she was worth.

Where Are Your Dreams Going?

Dreams come in all sizes – big dreams, small dreams, and in-between dreams. They also can be stated within specific, measurable time frames: one week, three months, one year, five years, 10 years, or 25 years. Once your dreams become translated into career goals, some may be too big and complicated to operationalize; instead, they may frustrate you and thus lead you to abandon your dreams. Others may be too small to challenge you to achieve anything significant. Ideally, you want your dreams and goals to be big enough to motivate you to achieve greater things. For example, this may be your ultimate career dream:

> _Become President of the United States._

Maybe it's attainable but don't let it frustrate you for the next 30 years. Try restating it as this more realistic and manageable goal:

> _Within the next 10 years, become the head of a terrific organization that enables me to fully use my skills and abilities to change other people's lives._

The two goals are basically the same but the second one is restated in more manageable terms. You can visualize what career steps you need to make in order to move to the top of such an organization. For example, you may decide as a prerequisite to achieving this goal that you need to go back to school and get an accounting degree or an MBA. With the right amount of education, skills, connections, and drive, you may attain your 10-year goal. Eventually your organization just might become the country! The difference may be in the time frame – 30 years for the first goal and five years for the second goal. Whatever you do, don't abandon either goal, but at least get moving toward achieving the second goal within five years.

Let's take another example of setting realistic and manageable goals but in this case relate it to money. If you are 22 years old, perhaps this is your real dream:

> _Make $20 million by the age of 35._

Write yourself a check for $20 million and postdate it for your 35th, 50th, or 65th birthday. Then restate your objective as a more manageable step-by-step intermediate goal:

Increase my income by 20% a year over the next 10 years.

> **Without a plan of action for implementing your goals, your dreams are likely to remain unfulfilled fantasies and frustrations.**

In this case, you can at least measure your progress in achieving your goal. Understanding the importance of moving from objectives to planning to implementation, you should next work out a weekly plan of action for achieving your yearly targeted goal. Without a plan of action for implementing your goals, your dreams are likely to remain unfulfilled fantasies and you may become frustrated with having so many dashed dreams and hopes of a better career and lifestyle.

What's Your Behavioral Advantage?

Employers tend to favor candidates who are both purposeful and enthusiastic about their career and work. Enthusiasm is difficult to express unless you have a passion or purpose related to what you want to do.

Unfortunately, many job seekers make the mistake of communicating self-centered purposes or goals to employers. Rather, they should be developing work- or employer-centered goals that tell employers what they plan to do for the employer. Take, for example, these goals:

A telecommunication position.

A challenging position in public relations that will lead to career advancement.

Both forms of goals frequently appear at the beginning of many resumes. Reading between the lines, these are essentially self-centered goals. They tell employers what it is you want from them for yourself. In other words, you are saying the following:

I want this position because I want you to advance my career or because I want to make $10,000 more than in my current job.

That's understandable, much like our honest but stupid interviewee who wanted to make more money. You're basically another self-centered job seeker in search of a place to cut you more paychecks and extend benefits.

When you state an objective in such "me" terms, you basically tell an employer that he or she may have a nice platform from which you can realize your career goals. Okay. You want benefits from this job. But in exchange for what? So why should I hire you? So you can realize your career goals? So you can make more money on my payroll? So you can move on to another employer in six months with new skills and experience acquired through my company? Understandable, but that's not quite the way the world of employers works. That world is all about **exchanging** benefits.

> *The world of employers is all about exchanging benefits.*

The mind of the employer is very simple – the employer wants to hire people who will **add value** to the organization. He or she wants to know about your **behavioral advantage** in comparison to other candidates. Talk to me about your **benefits for me** before I tell you about my **benefits for you.** What are you likely to accomplish for me? If I hire you, how much money will I save or how much additional income will you generate for this company? What is your predictable pattern of productivity? How will you solve my problems and with what outcomes for our organization? Give me some proof that you will do what you say you will do – not just make promises with the latest keywords and jargon about performance. These are all employer-centered questions that beg answers from job seekers who are often preoccupied with self-centered "me" issues.

Three Steps to Setting Employer-Centered Goals

There's nothing really difficult about setting career goals or objectives. The major problem is making goal-setting a priority, allocating enough time to do it properly, and then just doing it. At least in reference to your job search, one of the best ways to set goals and identify a career objective is to go through a series of self-directed exercises for generating information about what it is you really want to do in the future. The remainder of this chapter focuses on developing your own unique career objective.

It's important that you start with your career or job objective because it helps give direction to your job search. It will eventually be incorporated in your resume and discussed during job interviews. It should emphasize that you are a **purposeful individual who achieves results**. It should combine your interests and skills with the employer's needs. In so doing, it becomes a work- or employer-centered rather than self-centered objective.

You will eventually want to develop a very succinct, one-sentence, 25-word objective. Doing so may take you many hours or days trying to refine what you really want to do. This is not something to take lightly. The more time you spend on specifying a career objective, the better organized and targeted will be your job search. One of the most thorough ways of developing a career objective is to follow this progressive three-step process:

1. Gather important data about your interests, skills, and abilities.

2. Project your values and preferences into the future.

3. Test and refine your objective against reality.

Each step includes a series of self-directed pencil and paper exercises as well as some external testing and the use of the Internet. When completed, you should be able to produce a very thoughtful work- or employer-centered objective that will serve you well when writing your resume, networking, and interviewing for jobs. Arming you with a renewed sense of purpose, this objective should give meaning to your whole job search and perhaps to your future work life.

Step 1

The first step is to gather information about yourself from others, tests, and you, yourself. Use the following resources for gathering such data:

A. From others: Ask three to five individuals whom you know well to evaluate you according to the questions in the "Strength Evaluation" form on page 23. Explain to these people that you plan to conduct a

Strength Evaluation

TO: _____

FROM: _____

I am going through a career assessment process and thought you would be an appropriate person to ask for assistance. Would you please candidly respond to the questions below? Your comments will be given to me by the individual designed below; s/he will not reveal your name. Your comments will be used for advising purposes only. Thank you.

What are my strengths?

What weak areas might I need to improve?

In your opinion, what do I need in a job or career to give me satisfaction?

Please return to: _____

job search, and that you would greatly appreciate their candid appraisal so you can gain a better understanding of your strengths and weaknesses from the perspectives of others. Make copies of this form and ask your evaluators to complete and return it to a designated third party who will share the information – but not the respondent's name – with you.

B. **From vocational tests:** Although we prefer self-generated data, vocationally oriented tests can help clarify, confirm, and translate your understanding of yourself into occupational directions. If you decide to use vocational tests, contact a professional career counselor who can administer and interpret the tests. They can be found through community colleges, local workforce development offices, and private testing and assessment companies. To locate a career professional near you, check out the websites of America's CareerInfoNet, the National Board of Certified Counselors, and the National Career Development Association: www.acinet.org/acinet, www.nbcc.org, and www.ncda.org, respectively. These websites also have many other useful career resources to help you in your job search. Also, examine the latest edition of Taddy Maddox's *Tests* (Pro-Ed) which includes over 2,000 assessment instruments. For career assessment, we recommend several of the following tests:

- *Myers-Briggs Type Indicator®*
- *Strong Interest Inventory®*
- *Self-Directed Search (SDS)*
- *Campbell Interest and Skill Survey*
- *Keirsey Character Sorter*
- *Birkman Method*
- *Enneagram*
- *FIRO-B*
- *California Psychological Inventory (CPI)*
- *16 Personality Factors Profile*
- *Edwards Personal Preference Schedule*
- *Kuder Occupational Interest Survey*
- *APTICOM*
- *Jackson Vocational Interest Survey*
- *Ramak Inventory*

- *Vocational Interest Inventory*
- *Career Assessment Inventory*
- *Temperament and Values Inventory*

C. **From yourself:** Numerous alternatives are available for you to practice redundancy. First, complete the following exercises for identifying your work values, job frustrations and dissatisfactions, things you love to do, things you enjoy most about work, and your preferred interpersonal environments.

My Work Values

I prefer employment which enables me to:

___ contribute to society	___ be creative
___ have contact with people	___ supervise others
___ work alone	___ work with details
___ work with a team	___ gain recognition
___ compete with others	___ acquire security
___ make decisions	___ make money
___ work under pressure	___ help others
___ use power and authority	___ solve problems
___ acquire new knowledge	___ take risks
___ be a recognized expert	___ work at own pace

Select four work values from the above list which are the most important to you and list them in the space below. List any other work values (desired satisfactions) which were not listed above but are nonetheless important to you:

1. _____

2. _____

3. _____

4. _____

_____

Second, develop a comprehensive list of your past and present **job frustrations and dissatisfactions**. This should help you identify negative factors you should avoid in future jobs.

My Job Frustrations and Dissatisfactions

List as well as rank order as many past and present things that frustrate or make you dissatisfied and unhappy in job situations:

                                                                    Rank

1. _____   _____
2. _____   _____
3. _____   _____
4. _____   _____
5. _____   _____
6. _____   _____
7. _____   _____
8. _____   _____
9. _____   _____
10. _____   _____

Third, list at least ten things you most enjoy about work and rank each item accordingly:

Ten Things I Enjoy the Most About Work

                                                                    Rank

1. _____   _____
2. _____   _____
3. _____   _____
4. _____   _____
5. _____   _____
6. _____   _____
7. _____   _____
8. _____   _____
9. _____   _____
10. _____   _____

Fourth, you should also identify the types of interpersonal environments you prefer working in. Do this by specifying the types of people you like and dislike associating with:

Interpersonal Environments

Characteristics of people I like working with:	Characteristics of people I dislike working with:
1. _____	_____
2. _____	_____
3. _____	_____
4. _____	_____
5. _____	_____
6. _____	_____
7. _____	_____
8. _____	_____
9. _____	_____
10. _____	_____

Step 2

Project your values and preferences into the future by completing these simulation and creative thinking exercises:

A. $30 Million Lottery Exercise: First, assume that you have just won a $30 million lottery; now you don't have to work. After taxes, you have $20 million to work with. You decide the first $10 million will be for your use only – no giveaways or charities. What will you do with your time? At first? Later on? Second, you decide to give away the remaining $10 million. What kinds of causes, organizations, charities, etc. would you support? Complete the following form in which you answer these questions:

What Will I Do With $20 Million?

First $10 million is restricted to my use only:

_____

_____

_____

Second $10 million will be given away:

_____

_____

_____

B. Obituary Exercise: Make a list of the most important things you
would like to do or accomplish before you die. You can identify your
"to do" list two different ways. First, make a list in response to this
lead-in statement: *"Before I die, I want to..."*

Before I Die, I Want to . . .

1. _____

   _____

2. _____

   _____

3. _____

   _____

4. _____

   _____

5. _____

   _____

6. _____

   _____

7. _____

_____

8. _____

_____

9. _____

_____

10. _____

_____

Second, write a newspaper article which is actually your obituary for 10 years from now. Stress your accomplishments over the coming 10-year period.

My Obituary

Obituary for Mr./Ms. _____ to appear in the _____ Newspaper in 20____.

_____

_____

_____

_____

_____

_____

_____

_____

_____

_____

_____

_____

_____

C. My Ideal Work Week: Starting with Monday, place each day of the week as the headings of seven sheets of paper. Develop a daily calendar with 30-minute intervals, beginning at 7am and ending at midnight. Your calendar should consist of a 118-hour week. Next, beginning at 7am on Monday (sheet one), identify the **ideal activities** you would enjoy doing, or need to do for each 30-minute segment during the day. Assume you are capable of doing anything; you have no constraints except those you impose on yourself. Furthermore, assume that your work schedule consists of 40 hours per week. How will you fill your time? Be specific.

My Ideal Work Week

Monday

am		pm	
7:00	_____	4:00	_____
7:30	_____	4:30	_____
8:00	_____	5:00	_____
8:30	_____	5:30	_____
9:00	_____	6:00	_____
9:30	_____	6:30	_____
10:00	_____	7:00	_____
10:30	_____	7:30	_____
11:00	_____	8:00	_____
11:30	_____	8:30	_____
Noon	_____	9:00	_____
12:30	_____	9:30	_____
p.m.		10:00	_____
1:00	_____	10:30	_____
1:30	_____	11:00	_____
2:00	_____	11:30	_____
2:30	_____	12:00	_____
3:00	_____	Continue for Tuesday, Wednesday, Thursday, and Friday	
3:30	_____		

D. My Ideal Job Description: Develop your ideal future job. Be sure you include:

- Specific interests you want to build into your job
- Work responsibilities
- Working conditions
- Earnings and benefits
- Interpersonal environment
- Working circumstances, opportunities, and goals

Description of My Ideal Job

_____

_____

_____

_____

_____

_____

_____

_____

_____

_____

_____

_____

_____

_____

_____

Use "My Ideal Job Specifications" on page 32 to outline your ideal job. After completing this exercise, synthesize the job and write a detailed paragraph which describes the kind of job you would most enjoy.

My Ideal Job Specifications

Job Interests	Work Responsibilities	Working Conditions	Earnings /Benefits	Circumstances / Opportunities / Goals

Step 3

Test your objective against reality. Refine it by conducting market research, force field analysis, library research, and informational interviews.

A. **Market Research:** Based upon all other assessment activities, make a list of what you **do** or **make**:

Products/Services I Do or Make

1. _____
2. _____
3. _____
4. _____
5. _____

B. **Conduct Online and Library Research:** Research should strengthen and clarify your objective. Consult various reference materials on alternative jobs and careers. Most of these resources are available in print form at your local library or bookstore. Some are available in electronic versions online. If you explore the numerous company profiles and career sites available on the Internet, you should be able to tap into a wealth of information on alternative jobs and careers. Two of the best resources for initiating online research is Margaret Dikel's and Frances Roehm's *The Guide to Internet Job Searching* and Richard N. Bolles's *Job Hunting On the Internet.* For directories to key employment websites, see Ron and Caryl Krannich, *America's Top Internet Job Sites* and *The Directory of Websites for International Jobs;* Bernard Haldane Associates's, *Haldane's Best Employment Websites for Professionals;* and Peter Weddle's *WEDDLE's Directory of Employment-Related Internet Sites.* Many of the resources traditionally found in libraries are available online. The following websites function as excellent gateway sites, online databases, and research tools:

- CEO Express   ceoexpress.com
- Hoover's Online   hoovers.com

- Dun and Bradstreet's
  Million Dollar Database   dnbmdd.com/mddi
- Corporate Information   corporateinformation.com
- BizTech Network   brint.com
- AllBusiness   www.allbusiness.com
- BizWeb   bizweb.com
- Business.com   business.com
- Newspapers USA   www.newspapers.com
- Salary.com   salary.com
- Annual Report Service   annualreportservice.com
- Bloomberg   bloomberg.com
- Chamber of Commerce   chamberofcommerce.com
- CNN Money   http://money.cnn.com
- Daily Stocks   dailystocks.com
- The Corporate Library   thecorporatelibrary.com
- Forbes Lists   forbes.com/lists
- Fortune 500   fortune.com
- Harris InfoSource   www.harrisinfo.com
- Inc. 500   inc.com/500
- Moodys   www.moodys.com
- Motley Fool   fool.com
- NASDAQ   nasdaq.com
- One Source Corp Tech   onesource.com
- Standard & Poors   standardandpoors.com
- The Street   thestreet.com
- Thomas Register   thomasnet.com

Career, Job, and Employer Alternatives

- *25 Jobs That Have It All*
- *50 Cutting Edge Jobs*
- *Almanac of American Employers*
- *Almanac of American Employers Mid-Size Firms*
- *Enhanced Guide for Occupational Exploration*
- *Guide to Occupational Exploration*
- *Quick Prep Careers*
- *Occupational Outlook Handbook*
- *Occupational Outlook Quarterly*
- *O*NET Dictionary of Occupational Titles*

Industrial Directories

- *Dun and Bradstreet's Middle Market Directory*
- *Dun and Bradstreet's Million Dollar Directory*
- *Encyclopedia of Business Information Sources*
- *Geography Index*
- *Poor's Register of Corporations, Directors, and Executives*
- *Standard Directory of Advertisers*
- *The Standard Periodical Directory*
- *Standard and Poor's Industrial Index*
- *Standard Rate & Data Business Publications Directory*
- *Thomas' Register of American Manufacturers*

Associations

- *Encyclopedia of Associations*
- *National Trade and Professional Associations*
- Access thousands of associations online through: Ipl.org/ref/ AON and www.asaenet.org.

Government Sources

- *The Book of the States*
- *Congressional Directory*
- *Congressional Staff Directory*
- *Congressional Yellow Book*
- *Federal Directory*
- *Federal Yellow Book*
- *Municipal Yearbook*
- *Taylor's Encyclopedia of Government Officials*
- *United Nations Yearbook*
- *United States Government Manual*
- *Washington Information Directory*

Newspapers

- Major city newspapers and trade newspapers. Many are available online through these gateway sites: Ipl.org/reading/ news, newsdirectory.com, and newspaperlinks.com,
- Your targeted city newspaper – the Sunday edition.

Business Publications

- *Business 2.0, Business Week, Economist, Fast Company, Inc., Forbes, Fortune, Harvard Business Review, Newsweek, Smart Money, Time, U.S. News and World Report, Wired.* Many of these and other business-oriented publications can be viewed online through this terrific website: CEOExpress.com.
- Annual issues of publications surveying the best jobs and employers for the year: *Money, Fortune, Forbes,* and *U.S. News and World Report.* Several of these reports and publications are available online: money.com, fortune.com, and forbes.com/lists.

Other Library Resources

- Trade journals
- Publications of Chambers of Commerce; state manufacturing associations; and federal, state, and local government agencies
- Telephone books – The Yellow Pages
- Trade books on "how to get a job" (see order form at the end of this book and www.impactpublications.com)

C. **Conduct Informational Interviews:** This may be the most useful way to clarify and refine your objective. We'll discuss this procedure in Chapter 6 when we focus on the whole networking process related to finding a job.

After completing these steps, you will have enlarged your thinking to include what it is you would like to do (aspirations), and probed the realities of implementing your objective. Thus, setting a realistic work objective is a function of the diverse considerations outlined on page 37.

Your strongest emphasis should be on your competencies. Your work objective is realistic in that it is tempered by your past experiences, accomplishments, skills, and current research. An objective formulated in this manner permits you to think beyond your past experiences.

Objective Setting Process

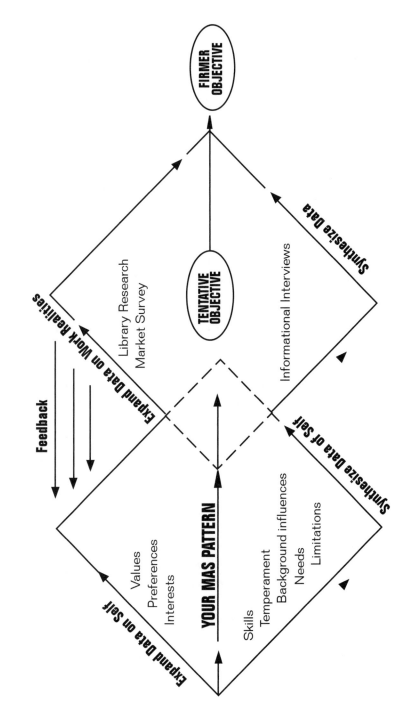

State a Functional Objective

Your job objective should be oriented toward skills and results or outcomes. You can begin by stating a functional job objective at two different levels: a general objective and a specific one for communicating your qualifications to employers both on resumes and in interviews. Thus, this objective-setting process sets the stage for other key job search activities. For the general objective, begin with the statement:

Stating Your General Objective

I would like a job where I can use my ability to _____which will result in _____.

The objective in this statement is both a **skill** and an **outcome**. For example, you might state:

Skills-Based and Results-Oriented Objective

I would like a job where my experience in food and beverage management, supported by excellent customer relations and negotiation skills, will result in a significant increase in clientele and a more profitable organization.

At a second level you may wish to re-write this objective to target various hospitality firms. For example, on your resume it becomes:

Job-Targeted Objective

An increasingly responsible F&B position, where proven management abilities and negotiation skills will be used for expanding the profitability and performance of the company.

The following are examples of weak and strong objective statements presented in various styles:

Weak Objectives

A challenging food and beverage position with a leading hotel that will provide opportunities for career advancement.

A position in security services which will allow me to work with people and maintain high security standards.

———————

A position in Sales with a progressive firm.

———————

A Dental Hygiene position with opportunity for advancement.

———————

Stronger Objectives

*To use innovative **landscape design** training for developing award-winning approaches to designing commercial properties.*

———————

A public relations position focused on developing and implementing programs, organizing people and events, and communicating positive ideas and images. Effective in public speaking and in managing publicity/promotional campaigns.

———————

A position as a General Sales Representative with a pharmaceutical house which will use chemistry background and ability to work on a self-directed basis in managing a marketing territory.

———————

A position in banking where skills in sales, accounts management, and customer relations will result in a high retention rate of current clients and a rapid increase in new customers.

———————

Retail Management position which will use sales/customer service experience and abilities to produce innovative displays and creative merchandising approaches. Long term goal: Merchandise Manager with corporate-wide responsibilities for promoting product lines.

———————

Responsible position in investment research and analysis, using skills in securities analysis, financial planning, and portfolio management. Long range goal: Chartered Financial Analyst.

It is important to relate your objective to your audience – employers. While you want a good paying job, employers want to know what you can do for them in exchange for a good paying job.

Your objective says something very important about how you want to conduct your life with the employer. It gives them an important indicator of the value you will bring to this job. Most important of all, it tells them who you really are in terms of your key values and accomplishments – a short answer to the big question of *"Why should I hire you?"*

3

Harbor Self-Defeating and Bad Attitudes

THERE IS AN OLD SAYING IN sports, business, and other fields that "attitude is everything." Not quite, but attitude definitely is important when it comes to the world of work and achieving success. Much of attitude has to do with perceptions and self-motivation. For example, when you drink half a glass of water, is the glass half empty or half full? Or when you get up to go to work on Monday morning, are you excited to start out the week to get lots accomplished or do you dread having to put in the first eight hours of another 40-hour workweek? Attitude often speaks to you in the form of that little inner voice that tells you that you can get things done and succeed. If you approach your job search and your job with a positive "can do" attitude, chances are that attitude will help energize and motivate you to achieve positive things.

Run With Winners

Unfortunately, many job seekers and employees seem to have negative or bad attitudes about their work. They often hang around people who have similar attitudes. Many of them have a "can't do" attitude – always find an excuse for not taking action – *I can't do that; I'll fail; it won't work;*

I've tried it before; I'll probably get rejected; it's a lot of trouble; or *I really don't want to do that.* Their friends and family may have similar negative attitudes – *you're not qualified; you'll never succeed; you shouldn't do that; that's not a good idea; leave it alone; that sounds like a lot of trouble; what happens if it doesn't work out?; I would be careful what you said; they will probably take advantage of you; why don't you just stay here and forget about it?* These "can't do" people will drag you down to their level, which is often one of low achievement, low self-esteem, and inertia. They do nothing to motivate you to take risks and achieve success. Instead, your success may threaten them, since they really don't want you to be successful!

> "Can't do" people will drag you down to their level. They really don't want you to succeed.

Attitudes are often infectious. If you want to get ahead and be successful, you are well advised to associate with people who have a positive "can do" attitude. Many of them are natural entrepreneurs and achievers. Both their outlook and language are positive. Rather than make excuses for not taking positive action, they have reasons for taking action which are often related to their goals.

What's Your Attitude Like?

Respond to the following statements by indicating your agreement or disagreement with each:

		Yes	No
1.	Other people often make my work difficult.	❑	❑
2.	If I get into trouble, it probably won't be my fault.	❑	❑
3.	I feel people often take advantage of me.	❑	❑
4.	People less qualified than me often get promoted at work.	❑	❑
5.	I avoid taking risks because I'm afraid of failing.	❑	❑
6.	I don't trust many of the people I work with.	❑	❑
7.	Not many people I work with take responsibility.	❑	❑

 8. Most people get ahead because of connections, schmoozing, and office politics.   ❏   ❏

 9. At work I'm often assigned more than other people in similar positions.   ❏   ❏

10. I expect to be discriminated against in the job search and on the job.   ❏   ❏

11. I don't feel like I can change many things.   ❏   ❏

12. I should have been promoted a long time ago.   ❏   ❏

13. I usually have to do the work myself rather than rely on others to get things done.   ❏   ❏

14. People often pick on me.   ❏   ❏

15. Employers try to take advantage of job seekers by offering them low salaries.   ❏   ❏

16. I don't like many of the people I work with.   ❏   ❏

17. There's not much I can do to get ahead.   ❏   ❏

18. My ideas are not really taken seriously.   ❏   ❏

19. I often think of reasons why my boss's and co-workers' ideas won't work.   ❏   ❏

20. I sometimes respond to suggestions by saying *"Yes, but...," "I'm not sure...," "I don't think it will work...," "Let's not do that..."*   ❏   ❏

21. Customers are often wrong but I have to put up with them nonetheless.   ❏   ❏

22. I don't see why I need to go for more training.   ❏   ❏

23. I often wish my boss would just disappear.   ❏   ❏

24. I sometimes feel depressed at work.   ❏   ❏

25. I have a hard time getting motivated at work.   ❏   ❏

26. I don't look forward to going to work on Monday.   ❏   ❏

27.	Friday is my favorite workday.	❏ ❏
28.	I sometimes come to work late or leave early.	❏ ❏
29.	My current job doesn't reflect my true talents.	❏ ❏
30.	I should have advanced a lot further in my career than my current position and salary indicate.	❏ ❏
31.	I'm worth a lot more than most employers are willing to pay.	❏ ❏
32.	I sometimes do things behind my boss's back that could get me into trouble.	❏ ❏

TOTALS   ___ ___

Not all of these statements necessarily reflect bad attitudes. Some may be honest assessments of how a company operates in practice. Indeed, some organizations have dysfunctional environments that breed negative attitudes. However, if you checked "Yes" to more than six of the statements, chances are you may be harboring some bad attitudes that affect both your job search and your on-the-job performance. You may want to examine these attitudes as possible barriers to getting ahead in your job search as well as on the job.

Excuses, Excuses, Excuses

Many negative and dysfunctional attitudes are related to excuses we make for bad behavior. Take, for example, the following list of "100 Excuses for Choosing Poor Behavior" compiled by Rory Donaldson on www.brains arefun.com. While many of these excuses apply to schoolchildren, many also relate to everyone else, including the elderly. He prefaces this list with Rudyard Kipling's observation that *"We have forty million reasons for failure, but not a single excuse":*

1. It's your fault.
2. I'm not happy.
3. It's too hot.
4. I'm too busy.
5. I'm sad.
6. I didn't sleep well.
7. It's not fair.
8. I wanted to watch TV.
9. I didn't write it down.
10. It's too hard.
11. It's too far away.
12. The teacher didn't explain it.
13. I forgot.
14. The dog was sick.

15. There was too much traffic.
16. I tried.
17. My pencil broke.
18. My grandmother wouldn't let me.
19. You're mean.
20. I didn't know it was today.
21. I'm too tired.
22. My brother was sick.
23. The car broke down.
24. It was snowing.
25. I hurt my foot.
26. I thought it was due tomorrow.
27. The ice was too thin.
28. I ran out of time.
29. I hurt my finger.
30. I don't feel well.
31. You didn't tell me.
32. It was cold.
33. I'm not good at that.
34. I left it in my pocket.
35. He made a face at me.
36. I wasn't.
37. I was rushed.
38. You didn't give it to me.
39. We did that last year.
40. That's not the way we learned at school.
41. His mother said it was O.K.
42. I already did it.
43. It was right here.
44. It's too much work.
45. It stinks.
46. I didn't know it was sharp.
47. I was scared.
48. I was frustrated.
49. I did already.
50. It wasn't in the dictionary.
51. I lost it.
52. Nobody likes me.
53. I have poor self esteem.
54. I'm too happy.
55. I'm sleepy.
56. He hit me.
57. I already know that.
58. I left it at school.
59. It's too easy.
60. It's not important.
61. I couldn't get in to my locker.
62. I dropped it.
63. I have a learning disorder.
64. I lost my pencil.
65. My pen leaked.
66. I have an excuse.
67. It got wet.
68. It got dirty.
69. My dog threw up.
70. I missed the bus.
71. I have a different learning style.
72. It was raining.
73. My grandfather was visiting.
74. I didn't know.
75. No one told me.
76. I don't have to.
77. My neck hurts.
78. I ran out of paper.
79. The electricity went out.
80. I don't know how.
81. I can't.
82. I don't know where it is.
83. He hit me first.
84. It's the weekend.
85. I ran out of money.
86. I'm too stupid.
87. My teacher said to do it this way.
88. I watched it at my friend's house.
89. I just cleaned it.
90. My friend got one.
91. You lost it.
92. It takes too much time.
93. He told me I didn't have to.
94. I'm hungry.
95. I couldn't open the door.
96. I'm too important.
97. It spilled.
98. I ran out of batteries.
99. I'm doing something else.
100. I didn't know it was hot.

Here are 20 additional excuses we and others have frequently encountered in the workplace. Some are even used by candidates during a job interview to explain their on-the-job behavior! Most of these excuses reflect an attitude lacking in responsibility and initiative:

1. No one told me.	11. I don't know how to do it.
2. I did what you said.	12. That's your problem.
3. Your directions were bad.	13. It wasn't very good.
4. It's not my fault.	14. Maybe you did it.
5. She did it.	15. I thought I wrote it down.
6. It just seemed to happen.	16. That's not my style.
7. It happens a lot.	17. He told me to do it that way.
8. What did he say?	18. I've got to go now.
9. I had a headache.	19. Where do you think it went?
10. I don't understand why.	20. We can talk about it later.

People with a positive attitude and proactive behavior don't engage in behaviors that reflect such excuses. They have a "can do" attitude that helps focus their goals on doing those things that are most important to achieving their goals. For example, rather than show up 10 minutes late for a job interview and say they got lost or had bad directions, people with a positive attitude and proactive behavior scope out the interview location the day before in anticipation of arriving 10 minutes early. They make no excuses because they engage in no-excuses behavior!

Change Your Attitudes

If you have negative attitudes and often need to make excuses for your behavior, it's time you took control of both your attitudes and behaviors. Start by identifying several of your negative attitudes and try to transform them into positive attitudes. For starters, examine these sets of negative and positive attitudes that can arise at various stages of the job search, especially during the critical job interview:

Negative Attitude	Positive Attitude
I didn't like my last employer.	It was time for me to move on to a more progressive company.
I haven't been able to find a job in over three months. I really want this one.	I've been learning a great deal during the past several weeks of my job search.

My last three jobs were problems.	I learned a great deal about what I really love to do from those last three jobs.
Do you have a job?	I'm in the process of conducting a job search. Do you know anyone who might have an interest in someone with my qualifications?
I can't come in for an interview tomorrow since I'm interviewing for another job. What about Wednesday? That looks good.	I have a conflict tomorrow. Wednesday would be good. Could we do something in the morning?
Yes, I flunked out of college in my sophomore year.	After two years in college I decided to pursue a career in computer sales.
I really hated studying math.	Does this job require math?
Sorry about that spelling error on my resume. I was never good at spelling.	(Doesn't point it out; if asked, say *"It's one that got away!"*)
I don't enjoy working in teams.	I work best when given an assignment that allows me to work on my own.
What does this job pay?	How does the pay scale here compare with other firms in the area?
Will I have to work weekends?	What are the normal hours for someone in this position?
I have to see my psychiatrist once a month. Can I have that day off?	I have an appointment I need to keep the last Friday of each month. Would it be okay if I took off three hours that day?
I'm three months pregnant. Will your health care program cover my delivery?	Could you tell me more about your benefits, such as health and dental care?

Can you think of any particular negative attitudes you might have that you can restate in positive language? Identify five that relate to your job search and work. State them in both the negative and positive:

	Negative Attitude	**Positive Attitude**
1.	_____	_____
	_____	_____
	_____	_____
2.	_____	_____
	_____	_____
	_____	_____
3.	_____	_____
	_____	_____
	_____	_____
4.	_____	_____
	_____	_____
	_____	_____
5.	_____	_____
	_____	_____
	_____	_____

Resources for Changing Attitudes

You'll find numerous books, audiotapes, videos, and software specializing in developing positive thinking. Most are designed to transform the thinking and perceptions of individuals by changing negative attitudes. One of the major themes underlying these products is that **you can change your life through positive thinking**. Individuals whose lives are troubled, for example, can literally transform themselves by changing their thinking in new and positive directions. These products are especially popular with individuals in sales who must constantly stay motivated and positive in the face of making cold calls that result in numerous rejections – an analogous situation many job seekers find themselves in when marketing themselves to employers. Positive thinking helps them get through the day, the week, and the month despite numerous rejections that would normally dissuade most people from continuing to pursue more sales calls that result in even more rejections.

One of the most important books on self-transformation through positive thinking is Napoleon Hill's *Think and Grow Rich*. This single book has had a tremendous influence on the development of the positive thinking industry which now includes hundreds of motivational speakers and gurus who produce numerous seminars, books, and audio programs for the true believers on everything from entrepreneurship and personal relationships to religion. Some of the most popular such gurus and their books include:

Napoleon Hill	▪ *Success Through a Positive Mental Attitude*
Dr. Norman Vincent Peale	▪ *Power of Positive Thinking*
	▪ *Six Attitudes for Winners*
Anthony Robbins	▪ *Personal Power*
	▪ *Unlimited Power*
	▪ *Awaken the Giant Within*
	▪ *Live With Passion!*
Keith Harrell	▪ *Attitude Is Everything*
Joel Osteen	▪ *Your Best Life Now*
Dr. Robert H. Schuller	▪ *Don't Throw Away Tomorrow*
	▪ *Be Happy Attitudes*
Dale Carnegie	▪ *How to Win Friends and Influence People*
Brian Tracy	▪ *Create Your Own Future*
	▪ *Goals!*
	▪ *Maximum Achievement*
David Schwartz	▪ *The Magic of Thinking Big*
Zig Ziglar	▪ *How to Get What You Want*
Og Mandino	▪ *Secrets of Success*
Steve Chandler	▪ *100 Ways to Motivate Yourself*
	▪ *Reinventing Yourself*
Bay and Macpherson	▪ *Change Your Attitude*

Any of these books will get you started on the road to changing your attitudes as well as your life. They are filled with fascinating stories of self-transformation, motivational language, and exercises for developing positive attitudes for success. You'll be much wiser in your job search, and on your job, if you read and re-read a few of these motivational books.

4

Fail to Do First Things First

OST JOB SEEKERS PUT THE cart before the horse. When
starting to look for a job, they tend to first focus on their
resume. They believe an effective job search basically starts
with writing a resume and then proceed to looking for job
listings, and then responding to vacancies with resumes and cover letters.
Approaching the job search in this manner, they spend a great deal of
time waiting to hear from employers whom they expect will respond to
their resume and letter.

While this may be the conventional, and seemingly logical, way of
organizing a job search, it's the wrong sequence of job search activities.
Writing a resume and responding to job listings should only come **after**
other critical stages in the job search have been completed. As you will
quickly learn, waiting is not a good job search strategy!

A 10-Step Job Search Process

Doing first things first when looking for a job involves understanding and
implementing a well-defined seven-step job search process. As we noted

50

in Chapter 1 when discussing a sequence of multiple job search errors, an effective job search follows the 10 steps outlined on page 52. Each step should be done in sequence. For example, writing resumes and letters should take place only **after** you have examined your attitudes and motivation (#1), become proactive (#2), selected job search approaches (#3), identified your motivated abilities and skills (#4), specified your goals (#5), and conducted research (#6). After completing your resume and letters, you should be well prepared to network (#8), interview (#9), and negotiate salary (#10). But if you start writing your resume and letters and responding to job listings without first dealing with your attitudes and motivations, identifying your skills and abilities, specifying your goals, and conducting research, chances are you will write weak resumes and letters, and your job search may lack focus. You'll eventually get a job, but it won't be one that best reflects your objective, skills, abilities, and pattern of accomplishments.

The Steps and Mistakes

Let's briefly examine each of the job search steps. Not surprisingly, many job search books have been written on each phase. Most such books focus on resumes, cover letters, interviews, salary negotiations, networking, assessment, goal setting, and research. Numerous do's and don'ts, as well as mistakes, are associated with each of these steps.

Identify Your Skills and Abilities

What exactly do you do well and enjoy doing? Can you quickly summarize your major accomplishments as evidence of your qualifications and behavioral advantage? This set of job search activities generates a critical language of action verbs and keywords for communicating your qualifications to employers. Here you identify what you do well and enjoy doing – your key strengths centered around an analysis of your accomplishments. Once you complete this step, you'll be able to clearly communicate to employers your pattern of performance – skills, abilities, and expected benefits or outcomes. We address this critical step in Chapter 6.

10 Steps to Job Search Success

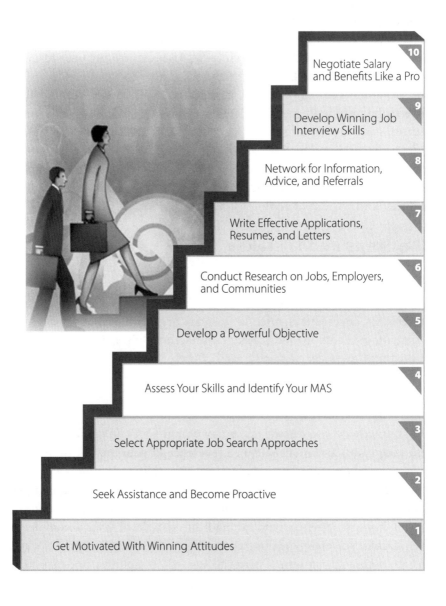

10 Negotiate Salary and Benefits Like a Pro

9 Develop Winning Job Interview Skills

8 Network for Information, Advice, and Referrals

7 Write Effective Applications, Resumes, and Letters

6 Conduct Research on Jobs, Employers, and Communities

5 Develop a Powerful Objective

4 Assess Your Skills and Identify Your MAS

3 Select Appropriate Job Search Approaches

2 Seek Assistance and Become Proactive

1 Get Motivated With Winning Attitudes

Specify Your Goals

We've already examined this step in Chapter 2. Once you know exactly what you want to do, and you specify your goals in employer-centered terms, you are a long way toward focusing your job search around exactly what you want to do. You should be able to communicate with enthusiasm your particular passion for work. Employers will know exactly what you want to do for them.

Conduct Research

We already identified key sources, including online resources, in Chapter 2 when we discussed the importance of conducting research as part of your objective-setting process (pages 33-36). Research is something that should be ongoing from the first day to the last day of your job search. It involves learning about companies, employers, jobs, careers, and the job search process. A good starting point for exploring careers, for example, is the biannual *Occupational Outlook Handbook* and *The O*NET Dictionary of Occupational Titles*. Both directories are available in book form as well as online:

Occupational Outlook Handbook   www.bls.gov/oco
O*NET Dictionary of
     Occupational Titles   http://online.onetcenter.org

Write and Distribute Resumes and Letters

Resumes and letters don't get jobs – they advertise you for job interviews. Writing and distributing resumes lie at the heart of any job search. When done right and in sequence with other job search steps, a powerful resume and letter clearly communicate what you have done, can do, and will do in the future for the employer. They provide evidence of your behavioral advantage. However, many job seekers make numerous mistakes related to writing and distributing resumes and letters. We discuss these mistakes as well as offer advice on how to develop dynamite resumes and letters in Chapter 9.

Network

While most job seekers spend a disproportionate amount of time responding to job listings in the advertised job market, they should be spending
more of their time on developing and implementing an effective networking campaign centered around the use of the informational interview. The
key to getting a job is knowing how to network for information, advice,
and referrals in order to uncover opportunities in the hidden job market.
As networking clearly demonstrates, success in finding a job is often more
a function of who you know than what you know. In Chapter 6 we
address the whole issue of networking in reference to the larger job search
process. We outline the importance of identifying, developing, building,
and nurturing your network for job and career success.

Interview

The job interview is the single most important step in the job search
process – no interview, no job. However, many job seekers make numerous mistakes relating to the job interview. We examine the major mistakes in Chapter 8 as well as outline how to improve your interview skills
in order to go on to win the job.

Negotiate Salary

Most job seekers make numerous mistakes relating to salary, from prematurely discussing the subject to not knowing what they are really worth in
today's job market. Many accept the very first offer without negotiating
compensation and other terms of employment. Others expect salaries that
have no basis except wishful thinking. Chapter 13 focuses on the many
mistakes job seekers make relating to salaries. It offers useful tips for
improving your salary negotiation skills.

Properly Sequence Your Job Search

How long should it take to complete your job search? That's always a
difficult question to answer because landing a job often seems like selling
a house – it can take a day, a week, a month, three months, or six months.
Success depends on your situation, potential buyers in the market, and

the amount of time you devote to selling yourself. Executive-level candidates, for example, often take longer because their job search is very focused on a few high-end jobs and they often work through executive recruiters. On average, however, expect to take two to four months to complete a well organized job search. You can shorten your job search time by accelerating various job search activities as outlined in the chart on page 56.

Our chart of job search activities emphasizes the importance of initiating each job search step in sequence. It also emphasizes that many job search activities, such as research and networking, should be ongoing activities. Indeed, the single most important activity for shortening your job search time will be **networking**. If you spend 40 to 60 hours a week networking for information, advice, and referrals, you'll soon be interviewing for real jobs. However, if you only spend a leisurely five to 10 hours a week networking, expect the number of invitations to job interviews to occur at a much slower pace. The choice is up to you. Throughout your job search, you are well advised to revisit the job search activity chart on page 52 to make sure you are fully engaged in conducting a well organized and effective job search. Above all, you want to be doing first things first.

Organization of Job Search Activities

Activity	Weeks																							
	1	2	3	4	5	6	7	8	9	10	11	12	13	14	15	16	17	18	19	20	21	22	23	24
Thinking, questioning, listening, evaluating, adjusting				██																				
Identifying abilities and skills			█																					
Setting objectives				█																				
Writing resume					█																			
Conducting research					████████████████████																			
Prospecting, referrals, networking					██																			
Interviewing										▬ ▬ ▬ ▬ ▬ ▬ ▬														
Receiving and negotiating job offers											▬ ▬ ▬ ▬ ▬ ▬ ▬											

5

Look for Jobs in the Wrong Places

WHERE WILL YOU LOOK FOR a job? Do you primarily survey job listings in newspapers and on the Internet? Will you post your resume online? What about developing an online portfolio and e-mailing your resume to prospective employers? Do you plan to make lots of cold calls to prospective employers, asking them if they have any vacancies? Have you considered attending job fairs and career conferences where you will have a chance to meet employers who are hiring? Ever considered hiring a so-called career professional to find you a job? What about signing up with temporary employment agencies? Are you planning to literally "spread the word" among family, friends, and acquaintances that you are looking for a job? Will you spend most of your job search time sending resumes and letters and waiting for employers to contact you?

Looking in All the Wrong Places

Most job seekers waste a great deal of time engaged in wishful thinking. They believe most available jobs are represented in newspaper classified ads or in job postings on Internet employment sites. As a result, they spend 80 percent of their time responding to such vacancy announcements with resumes and letters and then waiting to be contacted by employers for job interviews. Such activities give job seekers a false sense of making progress in the job market, because they believe they are doing something they think will result in a job. These also are the main job search activities of many frustrated job seekers who complain there no jobs available for them or that employers are not interested in hiring them. We hear this complaint again and again from job seekers who are primarily focused on finding employment through newspapers and the Internet.

But the likelihood of landing a job this way is similar to being struck by lightning – very unlikely. In fact, these are the least effective places to look for employment. Known as the "advertised job market," because employers pay to have their job vacancies listed in these media, these channels lead to job search success for only about 15 percent of job hunters.

Research continues to confirm that most jobs – over 80 percent – are found on the "hidden job market." These jobs are found through word-of-mouth, networking, cold calls, knocking on doors, and direct application. Jobs found on the hidden job market also tend to be better paying, more secure, less competitive, higher quality, and more satisfying than those found on the advertised job market. Advertised jobs are disproportionately competitive, difficult to fill, and low-paying positions. After all, employers often have to advertise a job because they find it is difficult to fill through other less public means.

Using Your Time Wisely

So how should you best use your job search time? The answer is simple but the advice is often difficult to follow. You should spend most of your job search time focused on the hidden job market. If you are devoting more than 30 percent of your time looking for jobs through classified ads and on the Internet, you are most likely wasting a great deal of job search time that could be put to more productive use by engaging in the most effective job search activities, especially networking and informational interviews. Your goal should be to get as many job interviews as possible – not to send out lots of resumes and letters in the hope of connecting to a few employers. As you will see once we examine networking in the next chapter, the fastest way to get job interviews is through networking for information, advice, and referrals.

Individuals with not-so-hot backgrounds should spend most of their job search time focused on the hidden job market. Networking and cold-calling activities enable them to be pre-screened by many individuals who will refer them to employers interested in their abilities and skills. Employers found on the hidden job market are less likely to rely on paper qualifications, which often accentuate red flags of applicants with difficult backgrounds. Through networking, you are screened more on the basis of face-to-face meetings and conversations, where what you say and do during the encounters are more important than what you have written in your resume, letters, and applications.

> _If you are spending more than 30 percent of your time looking for jobs through classified ads and the Internet, you are wasting time that could be put to more productive use._

Incorporate Many Approaches

There is no one best way to find a job since all methods work for different individuals. After all, with a little effort, anyone can find a job in a full employment economy. However, some approaches are more effective than others. If your goal is to find a very rewarding job that you do well and enjoy doing, you'll want to focus on methods that are more likely to result in such jobs. The question you should constantly ask yourself throughout your job search is this:

What is the most productive use of my time?

We strongly urge you to simultaneously use a variety of job finding approaches. If, for example, you only focus on responding to classified ads and Internet job postings, you'll be missing out on over 80 percent of potential jobs. You should incorporate several of these 13 methods in your job search:

1. Respond to classified ads
2. Apply to Internet job postings
3. Post a resume or portfolio online
4. Make cold calls to potential employers
5. Knock on doors or just show up at work sites
6. Send unsolicited e-mails to employers
7. Attend job fairs and career conferences
8. Network for information, advice, and referrals
9. Register with employment agencies and temporary job firms
10. Hire a career professional to locate employers
11. Contact executive job search firms
12. Advertise your availability for employment
13. Stand on day laborer corners so employers can find you

Useful Resources

The following books can assist you in incorporating a variety of approaches into your job search:

America's Top Internet Job Sites
Change Your Job, Change Your Life
e-Resumes (two books with this title)
A Foot in the Door
How to Get Interviews From Classified Job Ads
Job Hunting on the Internet
*Job Hunting Tips for People With Hot and Not-So-Hot
    Backgrounds*
Overcoming Barriers to Employment
The Savvy Networker
Shortcut Your Job Search
The Unwritten Rules of the Highly Effective Job Search
What Color Is Your Parachute?

These and many other related resources are available through Impact
Publications's online bookstore: www.impactpublications.com.

6

Hang Around the Wrong Crowds and Networks

CONDUCTING A SUCCESSFUL JOB search depends a great deal on the type of crowd you hang out with. Unfortunately, many job seekers either associate with the wrong crowd or they lack a useful crowd to hang out with altogether.

The crowd we're talking about is your network of relationships – your relatives, friends, colleagues, and acquaintances you interact with and who might be helpful in giving you information, advice, and referrals to enhance your job search. In a job search, we also focus on building new networks of relationships based upon referrals and cold calls. How well you identify, build, and nurture your networks throughout your job search will largely determine how successful you are in landing a job.

The Advertised and Hidden Job Markets

As we noted in Chapter 5, job seekers should be aware of two different job markets – advertised and hidden. Savvy job seekers know that advertised jobs – those found in classified ads of newspapers or posted on Internet sites – represent perhaps less than 30 percent of all jobs available at any time. Most jobs are unadvertised – found through word-of-mouth, employment firms, executive recruiters, or by knocking on doors. Found on what is called the "hidden job market," these jobs are often the best jobs available. They are usually less competitive than jobs in the advertised job market, and many of them pay better and have a very promising future.

Unfortunately, most job seekers mistakenly think that the majority of jobs are found on the advertised job market. As a result, they polish up their resume and letters and spend a disproportionate amount of their time responding to classified job ads in the newspaper. Internet-savvy job seekers shift their attention to job postings on the Internet, as if this high-tech media really makes a difference in the number and quality of jobs available. It's still the advertised job market characterized by high competition and frustration for most job seekers. Your chances of getting a good job on the advertised job market are not good. Indeed, you will most likely waste precious job search time chasing after nonexistent jobs in this

> *Your chances of getting a good job on the advertised job market are not good. The best and least competitive jobs are found on the hidden job market.*

market. Many job seekers who focus on this end of the job market spend a great deal of time waiting to hear good news in reference to their mailed, faxed, or emailed resumes and letters. The symbol of this type of job seeker is someone who waits, waits, and waits in frustration. Moving paper and emails gives them a false sense of making progress in this deceptive job market.

Savvy job seekers play the advertised job market game, but they know that most of the best and least competitive jobs are found on the hidden job market. Navigating through this job market requires interpersonal skills for acquiring information, advice, and referrals. Your goal should be to learn as much as possible about jobs appropriate for you that may or may not be advertised. In the process of networking, you communicate your interests, skills, and abilities to individuals in your network who refer you to other individuals who might be interested in giving you more advice and referrals. If you develop an active networking campaign that involves making five new contacts a day, you should quickly accelerate your job search. Best of all, you will soon be invited to job interviews which hopefully will turn into job offers.

Are You a Savvy Networker?

Savvy networkers know the importance of conducting a well organized job search that involves three critical networking activities: **connect** with others, **build** networks, and **nurture** relationships within those networks. Once you learn how to connect, build, and nurture your network, you should be able to quickly and successfully navigate the hidden job market.

Just how savvy are you when it comes to finding a job and advancing your career? Do you have the necessary networking skills for success? Can you quickly network your way to job and career success, or do you need to focus on developing specific networking skills? Let's start by testing your "Savvy Networking I.Q." You do this by responding to the following set of agree/disagree statements:

Your Savvy Networking I.Q.

INSTRUCTIONS: Respond to each statement by circling the number to the right that best represents your situation. The higher your score, the higher your "Savvy Networking IQ."

SCALE: 5 = strongly agree   2 = disagree
                4 = agree   1 = strongly disagree
                3 = maybe, not certain

1. I enjoy going to business and social functions where I have an opportunity to meet new people. (CONNECT/BUILD)   5   4   3   2   1

2. I usually take the initiative in introducing myself to people I don't know. (CONNECT)   5   4   3   2   1

3. I enjoy being in groups and actively participating in group activities. (CONNECT/BUILD)   5   4   3   2   1

4. On a scale of 1 to 10, my social skills are at least a "9." (BUILD/NURTURE)   5   4   3   2   1

5. I listen carefully and give positive
    feedback when someone is speaking
    to me. (CONNECT/BUILD)   5   4   3   2   1

6. I have a friendly and engaging
    personality that attracts others to me.
    (CONNECT/BUILD/NURTURE)   5   4   3   2   1

7. I make a special effort to remember
    people's names and frequently address
    them by their name. (CONNECT)   5   4   3   2   1

8. I carry business cards and often give
    them to acquaintances from whom I
    also collect business cards. (CONNECT)   5   4   3   2   1

9. I have a system for organizing business
    cards I receive, including notes on the
    back of each card. (BUILD)   5   4   3   2   1

10. I seldom have a problem starting a
    conversation and engaging in small
    talk with strangers. (CONNECT)   5   4   3   2   1

11. I enjoy making cold calls and persuading
    strangers to meet with me. (CONNECT)   5   4   3   2   1

12. I usually return phone calls in a timely
    manner. (CONNECT)   5   4   3   2   1

13. If I can't get through to someone on the
    phone, I'll keep trying until I do, even if it
    means making 10 more calls. (CONNECT)   5   4   3   2   1

14. I follow up on new contacts by phone,
    email, or letter. (BUILD)   5   4   3   2   1

15. I have several friends who will give me
    job leads. (BUILD)   5   4   3   2   1

16. I frequently give and receive referrals.
    (BUILD)   5   4   3   2   1

17. I have many friends. (BUILD)   5   4   3   2   1

18. I know at least 25 people who can give
    me career advice and referrals. (BUILD)   5   4   3   2   1

19. I don't mind approaching people with my professional concerns. (CONNECT/BUILD)   5   4   3   2   1

20. I enjoy having others contribute to my success. (BUILD)   5   4   3   2   1

21. When I have a problem or face a challenge, I usually contact someone for information and advice. (BUILD)   5   4   3   2   1

22. I'm good at asking questions and getting useful advice from others. (BUILD)   5   4   3   2   1

23. I usually handle rejections in stride by learning from them and moving on. (BUILD)   5   4   3   2   1

24. I can sketch a diagram, with appropriate linkages, of individuals who are most important in both my personal and professional networks. (BUILD)   5   4   3   2   1

25. I regularly do online networking by participating in social networks, mailing lists, chats, and bulletin boards. (CONNECT/BUILD)   5   4   3   2   1

26. I regularly communicate my accomplishments to key members of my network. (NURTURE)   5   4   3   2   1

27. I make it a habit to stay in touch with members of my network by telephone, email, and letter. (NURTURE)   5   4   3   2   1

28. I regularly send personal notes, birthday and holiday greeting cards, letters, and emails on special occasions to people in my network. (NURTURE)   5   4   3   2   1

29. I still stay in touch with childhood friends and old schoolmates. (NURTURE)   5   4   3   2   1

30. I have a great network of individuals whom I can call on at anytime for assistance, and they will be happy to help me. (BUILD/NURTURE)   5   4   3   2   1

31. I belong to several organizations,
    including a professional association.
    (CONNECT/BUILD)   5   4   3   2   1

32. I consider myself an effective networker
    who never abuses relationships.
    (CONNECT/BUILD/NURTURE)   5   4   3   2   1

33. Others see me as a savvy networker.
    (CONNECT/BUILD/NURTURE)   5   4   3   2   1

TOTAL I.Q.

If your total composite I.Q. is above 155, you're most likely a savvy networker. If you're below 120, you're probably lacking key networking skills. Each of the above items indicates a particular connect, build, or nurture behavior or skill that contributes to one's overall networking effectiveness. Concentrate on improving those skills on which you appear to be weak. For example, you may discover you are particularly savvy at "connecting" with people but you're weak on "building" and "nurturing" relationships – or vice versa – that define your network.

Key Networking Books

Numerous books can assist you in developing effective networking skills. While most such books focus on networking in all types of situations, these three books focus specifically on networking skills relevant to conducting an effective job search:

> *A Foot in the Door*
> *Information Interviewing*
> *Networking for Job Search and Career Success*
> *The Savvy Networker*
> *Shortcut Your Job Search*

Other popular networking books that focus on networking in many different business and social settings include the following:

Achieving Success Through Social Capital
Breakthrough Networking
Dig Your Well Before You're Thirsty
Endless Referrals
Fine Art of Small Talk
The Golden Rule of Schmoozing
Great Connections
How to Make People Like You in 90 Seconds or Less
How to Work a Room
Little Black Book of Connections
Make Your Contacts Count
Masters of Networking
Networking for Everyone
Networking Smart
Networking Survival Guide
Never Eat Along
One Phone Call Way
People Power
Power Networking
Power Schmoozing
The Power to Get In
The Secrets of Savvy Networking
Super Networking
Work the Pond!

Internet Resources for Networking

While a good book can be a terrific resource for developing networking skills, numerous Internet websites also are wonderful resources for understanding, developing, and practicing networking skills. We recommend visiting the following websites which deal with different aspects of networking, from joining an online career-related network to locating long-lost former classmates and friends whom you might want to contact as part of your network building activities:

Trendy websites for building networks for personal and professional purposes, from dating and making new friends to developing special communities for work and play:

- MySpace   www.myspace.com
- Facebook   www.facebook.com
- Friendster.com   www.friendster.com
- Orkut   www.orkut.com

Usenet newsgroups for online networking opportunities:

- Google   www.groups.google.com
- Topica   www.topica.com
- Yahoo!   http://groups.yahoo.com
- MSN   http://groups.msn.com
- Newzbot   www.newzbot.com
- Usenet Info Center   www.ibiblio.org/usenet-i/
                             home.html

Sites for finding, or creating, mailing lists related to your particular career interests:

- Coollist   coollist.com
- Google   groups.google.com
- Topica   topica.com
- Yahoo! Groups   groups.yahoo.com

Several employment sites have message boards to network for information, advice, and referrals. The largest and most comprehensive networking boards are found on Monster.com and Vault.com:

- Monster.com   http://networking.monster.com/
                             messageboards
- Vault.com   www.vault.com/community/mb/
                             mb_home.jsp

Sites with useful information and advice on how to sharpen your networking skills:

- WetFeet   wetfeet.com/advice/
                             networking.asp

- Quintessential Careers   quintcareers.com/networking.html
- Riley Guide   www.rileyguide.com/netintv.html
- WinningTheJob   www.winningthejob.com
- SchmoozeMonger   www.schmoozemonger.com
- Susan RoAne   susanroane.com/free.html
- Contacts Count   contactscount.com/articles.html

Directories to associations which function as important networking arenas for professionals:

- Associations on the Net   ipl.org/ref/AON
- American Society of
  Association Executives   www.asaenet.org
- GuideStar   guidestar.org

Major women's online networking groups:

- Advancing Women   advancingwomen.com
- American Association of
  University Women   aauw.org
- American Business
  Women's Association   abwahq.org
- Business Women's
  Network Interactive   www.bwni.com
- Federally Employed Women   few.org
- Systers   systers.org

Alumni groups for networking:

- Alumni.net   alumni.net
- Alumniconnections   bcharrispub.com/isd/alumniconnections.html
- Planet Alumni   planetalumni.com

Locators for finding old friends and re-building networks:

- Anywho   anywho.com

- Classmates   classmates.com
- InfoSpace   infospace.com
- Switchboard   switchboard.com
- The Ultimate White Pages   theultimates.com/white
- World Pages   worldpages.com
- Yahoo   people.yahoo.com

Military locators and buddy finders:

- GI Buddies.com   gibuddies.com
- GI Search.com   gisearch.com
- Military.com   military.com
- Military Connections   militaryconnections.com
- Military USA   militaryusa.com

Job search clubs and support groups:

- 5 O'Clock Clubs   fiveoclockclub.com
- 40-Plus Clubs   40plus.org/chapters
- ExecuNet   execunet.com
- Professionals in Transition   jobsearching.org

Watch Your Online Presence

Online social networking through such popular groups as Facebook.com and MySpace.com has potential downsides for many of today's naive job seekers. If you are participating in such networks, be very careful what you put online about yourself, especially any youthful indiscretions concerning alcohol, drugs, and sex or bad language and questionable ideas about work and life. Being ostensibly "cool" online in such social settings can come back to haunt you when looking for a job. Indeed, more and more employers report doing background checks on candidates by searching for them online through such sites as Facebook.com and MySpace.com.

Be sure to search for yourself online **before** applying for a position since a prospective employer will probably do so before inviting you to an interview or offering you a job. Start by doing Google, Yahoo, and MSN searches of your name to see if there is anything online about you that you will need to explain during a job interview. Also, inventory your online presence by checking on any online profiles you have created that could cause embarrassment or silent rejections. Put yourself in the shoes of a prospective employer who might view you or read about you online. Will what they see and read about you strengthen your candidacy? If not, this would be a good time to clean up your act by removing or restructuring your online presence.

Network Your Way to Job Success

Whatever you do, make sure you focus much of your job search attention on the hidden job market. Develop the necessary networking skills for acquiring useful information, advice, and referrals. If you launch an effective networking campaign, you should be able to significantly shorten your job search time. You'll meet many helpful individuals who can provide advice on how you can improve your job search. Best of all, these individuals will plug you into the word-of-mouth networks where the good jobs will be found.

If you spend much of your time responding to classified ads and online job postings with resumes and letters, you'll most likely become disappointed and frustrated with the results. Such misplaced job search emphasis is often responsible for the often-heard lament of the frustrated job seeker – *"No one will hire me!"* Indeed, if you use an approach that takes you in the wrong direction, you'll find few employers who want to hire you. But if you focus on your networks, especially those with job and career content, you may discover many people want to hire you!

7

Disregard Skills and Accomplishments

WHY WOULD AN EMPLOYER want to hire you, a stranger they know very little about? It's probably not because you're a nice person, you know someone important, you have a good education, you seem clever in a job interview, or you have a long resume. They hire people who they believe have the necessary knowledge, skills, and abilities to do the job in question. Above all, they want proof of your past accomplishments so they can predict your future performance with them. In other words, they want to know what **benefits**, in the form of specific accomplishments, you will likely generate for them should they hire you. Therefore, you need to tell a very compelling story about yourself that persuades employers to take a series of hiring actions – invite you to interviews and offer you jobs.

Tell Your Story

What exactly is your story? Is it a compelling story? Or do you primarily focus on listing individual jobs and education background on your resume? Do you have difficulty summarizing who you really are in terms of your past accomplishments and future goals? Are you uncertain how to develop a series of memorable two-minute stories about your work life?

While most job seekers communicate difference pieces of information about themselves to prospective employers, few of them can put together a coherent story about themselves. We each have stories about ourselves that can communicate to others our purpose and what we are especially talented at doing. These stories emphasize our goals, accomplishments, and motivated abilities and skills (MAS). They identify us as someone who is especially talented in doing certain things and who should be hired because you will likely achieve similar results with a new employer.

The best candidates know how to tell compelling stories about themselves in reference to the employer's needs. They are adept at telling and re-telling stories about what they have done, can do, and will do in the future. These stories appear in their resume and letters and are articulated during job interviews.

If you are not use to telling stories about yourself, it's time you begin making some changes in how you talk about yourself. Ask yourself what are the five most memorable stories about my accomplishments that will likely impress potential employers? Can I tell each of these stories within two minutes? Begin developing a set of two minute stories that should be represented on your resume and in letters as well as shared during your job interviews. Focus on stories that demonstrate your pattern of accomplishments. For example, instead of telling a prospective employer that you graduated from XYZ university with a B.A. in psychology, tell the interviewer why you decided to study psychology and how it relates to your career goals, including the job for which you are interviewing.

These two books can help you develop some great stories for writing your resume and preparing for the job interview:

The Story of You: And How to Create a New One
Tell Your Story, Win the Job

No Evidence of Accomplishments

Unfortunately, most job seekers are ill-equipped to talk about their accomplishments or behavioral advantage in comparison to other candidates. They usually think about formal job descriptions rather than actual **outcomes** of their work or behavior. Too often they approach employers without a good sense of what they have done, can do, and will do in the future. Instead, they tend to focus on the duties and responsibil-ities assigned to jobs they held rather than the knowledge, skills, and abilities they possessed in actually doing the job, which may be quite different from the position description. In fact, most job seekers define "Experience" on their resumes and in job interviews as formal duties and responsibilities rather than things they actually achieved – accomplish-ments – in the performance of their duties and responsibilities. They give little evidence of what they exactly accomplished in those positions. While employers understand job descriptions, they don't understand why candidates have difficulty articulating what they actually accomplished.

Take, for example, the following "Experience" statement that might appear on a resume:

Supervised a seven-person inventory management office.

Such a statement tells an employer nothing about your actual skills and accomplishments. It basically says you were a squatter – you held a posi-tion in which you were given the re-sponsibility of supervising other peo-ple. So what? Many people sit in such positions. The question is how did you stand and perform in reference to the employer's needs? What distin-guished your behavior from hundreds of other people in similar positions? Did you do well in that position? How well? With what effects? What exactly did you accomplish as a supervisor? Did you build an effective team that saved the company 20 percent in lost inventory? Were you given an award for your innovative inventory management system that reduced personnel costs by 30 percent? Or did you just occupy the position of "Supervisor" – you came to work, sat, gave orders, completed paperwork, and went home – with no distinguishing performance that separates you from the run-of-the-mill inventory managers?

> *The question is how did you stand and perform in reference to the employer's needs?*

If you define your "experience" as benefits, outcomes, or actual per-formance, you give an employer a very different and positive picture of your abilities and skills. Your accomplishments motivate employers to interview and hire you. Best of all, you help set the focus for discussing your future performance with the employer who interviews you. Instead of leaving yourself open to performance questions about your duties and responsibilities – _"Tell me what you did as inventory supervisor"_ – you focus the discussion on your past performance as it might relate to future accomplishments with the employer interested in your qualifications. The employer might ask you the following:

> _"I find that very interesting. Tell me more about how you were able to achieve a 30 percent reduction in personnel costs in just 24 months. Let's take a look at our inventory system here. Based upon what we've talked about thus far, what do you think you could do here about reducing costs?"_

Contrast these two different experience statements about formal responsibilities versus actual accomplishments:

Experience Expressed as Responsibilities

Supervised a seven-person inventory management office.

Experience Expressed as Accomplishments

As inventory manager in charge of a seven-person office, reduced operating costs by 20 percent and personnel costs by 30 percent within 24 months. Received the "Best Employee of the Year Award" for designing and implementing a model inventory management system that eliminated the need for one of three warehouses. Annual savings: $735,000.

These are two very different ways of presenting your qualifications and experience to employers. Which one do you think presents the best impression and thus makes the job seeker look more attractive to a potential employer? If you were choosing between two candidates who might be equally qualified in terms of experience, which candidate would you be more interested in interviewing – the one who communicates formal assigned responsibilities or the one who stresses actual accomplishments? Which one communicates a clear behavioral advantage? There's really no contest here: Employers are impressed with candidates who use the language of the employer – focus on their accomplishments in reference to the needs of employers.

Identify Your Skills

The first step to communicating your qualifications to employers in the form of accomplishments is to identify your skills. Most people have hundreds of skills, but they have difficulty identifying and articulating the ones that are most important to employers. Many skills are related to specific jobs, such as operating a particular piece of equipment or working in various software programs. We call these **work-content skills** because they tend to be technical in nature, require some form of training and education, and are specific to particular jobs. Many of these skills become keywords and core competencies employers look for on resumes and which job seekers stress as part of their technical qualifications. For example, an employer may be looking for someone who has these specific work-content skills: QuarkXpress, InDesign, PowerPoint, MS Word, Excel, Access, Lotus, C++, TMQ, spreadsheet, and Peachtree. Other skills tend to be more general and thus can be applied to many different jobs. We call these **functional** or **transferable skills**. For example, many job seekers possess these highly valued communication, organization, and decision-making skills:

> *Many skills become keywords and core competencies employers look for on resumes.*

- writing
- public speaking
- organization
- management
- leadership

- critical thinking
- dependability
- negotiating
- trouble-shooting
- supervision

Many people also possess several personal characteristics that are conducive to working in organizations and with groups:

- trustworthy
- punctual
- conscientious
- creative
- self-motivated
- reliable

- dependable
- patient
- resourceful
- responsible
- tenacious
- cooperative

These and many other transferable skills enable individuals to make job and career changes.

If you are a recent high school or college graduate and do not know what you want to do, you probably should take a battery of vocational tests and psychological inventories to identify your interests and skills. We identified several of these tests in Chapter 2 (pages 24-25). If you have a great deal of work experience, chances are you don't need complex testing. You have experience, you have well defined values, and you know what you don't like in a job. Therefore, we outline several alternative skills identification exercises – ranging from simple to complex – for assisting you at this stage. We recommend using the most complete and extensive activity – Motivated Abilities and Skills (MAS) Exercise – to gain a thorough understanding of your strengths.

Use the following exercises to identify both your work-content and transferable skills. These self-assessment techniques stress your positives or strengths rather than identify your negatives or weaknesses. They should generate a rich vocabulary for communicating your "qualifications" to employers. Each exercise requires different investments of your time and effort as well as varying degrees of assistance from other people.

Simple Checklist Method

Most functional/transferable skills can be classified into two general skills and trait categories – organizational/interpersonal skills and personality/ work-style traits. Review the following lists of transferable skills. Place a "1" in front of the skills that **strongly** characterize you; assign a "2" to those skills that describe you to a **large extent**; put a "3" before those that describe you to **some extent**. After completing this exercise, review the lists and rank order the 10 characteristics that best describe you on each list.

Organizational and Interpersonal Skills

__ communicating	__ trouble-shooting
__ problem solving	__ implementing
__ analyzing/assessing	__ self-understanding
__ planning	__ understanding
__ decision-making	__ setting goals
__ innovating	__ conceptualizing
__ thinking logically	__ generalizing

__ evaluating
__ identifying problems
__ synthesizing
__ forecasting
__ tolerating ambiguity
__ motivating
__ leading
__ selling
__ performing
__ reviewing
__ attaining
__ team building
__ updating
__ coaching
__ supervising
__ estimating
__ negotiating
__ administering

__ managing time
__ creating
__ judging
__ controlling
__ organizing
__ persuading
__ encouraging
__ improving
__ designing
__ consulting
__ teaching
__ cultivating
__ advising
__ training
__ interpreting
__ achieving
__ reporting
__ managing

Personality and Work-Style Traits

__ diligent
__ patient
__ innovative
__ persistent
__ tactful
__ loyal
__ successful
__ versatile
__ enthusiastic
__ outgoing
__ expressive
__ adaptable
__ democratic
__ resourceful
__ determining
__ creative
__ open
__ objective
__ warm
__ orderly
__ tolerant
__ frank
__ cooperative

__ honest
__ reliable
__ perceptive
__ assertive
__ sensitive
__ astute
__ risk taker
__ easygoing
__ calm
__ flexible
__ competent
__ punctual
__ receptive
__ diplomatic
__ self-confident
__ tenacious
__ discreet
__ talented
__ empathic
__ tidy
__ candid
__ adventuresome
__ firm

__ dynamic	__ sincere
__ self-starter	__ initiator
__ precise	__ competent
__ sophisticated	__ diplomatic
__ effective	__ efficient

Autobiography of Accomplishments

Write a lengthy essay about your life accomplishments. This could range from 20 to 100 pages. After completing the essay, go through it page by page to identify what you most enjoyed doing (working with different kinds of information, people, and things) and what skills you used most frequently as well as enjoyed using. Finally, identify those skills you wish to continue using. After analyzing and synthesizing this data, you should have a relatively clear picture of your strongest skills.

Motivated Abilities and Skills (MAS) Exercise

Short of sitting down with a trained career professional and undergoing a thorough career assessment, this is the most thorough-going and useful self-assessment exercise we have found. While it is somewhat complex and time-consuming, it's time and effort well spent. It generates a great deal of data on your abilities and skills and then synthesizes them in terms of your major strengths – those things you do well and enjoy doing. This is precisely the type of information you need on yourself in order to best communicate your strengths and accomplishments to employers on resume and letters and in interviews.

The focus of this exercise is identifying your motivated abilities and skills (MAS). The emphasis is on specifying your motivated abilities and skills rather than just coming up with a laundry list of abilities and skills. For example, while you may be a very good chef, you may not enjoy using all the wonderful abilities and skills that make you an excellent chef. Instead, you may discover what you really enjoy doing is organizing meetings and events and working with large groups of people – skills that served you well as a chef in the kitchen of a large hotel. Indeed, you may want to become a meetings planner rather than continue as a chef. Our MAS exercise, widely used by career counselors, is especially useful for those who feel they need a thorough analysis of their past achievements. Initially developed by Bernard Haldane Associates, this exercise is variously referred to as *Success Factor Analysis, System to Identify Motivated Skills,* or *Intensive Skills Identification.*

This technique helps you identify which skills you **enjoy** using. While you can use this technique on your own, it is best to work with someone else. Since you will need six to eight hours to properly complete this exercise, divide your time into two or three work sessions.

The exercise consists of six steps, involving generating raw data, identifying patterns, analyzing the data through reduction techniques, and synthesizing the patterns into a transferable skills vocabulary. You need strong analytical skills to complete this exercise on your own. The six steps include:

1. **Identify 15-20 achievements:** While ideally you should inventory over 100-150 achievements, let's start by focusing on a minimum of 15-20 achievements. These consist of things you enjoyed doing, believe you did well, and felt a sense of satisfaction, pride, or accomplishment in doing. You can see yourself performing at your best and enjoying your experiences when you analyze your achievements. This information reveals your motivations since it deals entirely with your voluntary behavior. In addition, it identifies what is right with you by focusing on your positives and strengths. Identify achievements throughout your life, beginning with your childhood. Your achievements should relate to specific experiences – not general ones – and may be drawn from work, leisure, education, military, or home life. Put each achievement at the top of a separate sheet of paper. For example, your achievements might appear as follows:

Sample Achievement Statements

"When I was 10 years old, I started a small paper route and built it up to the largest in my district."

"I started playing chess in ninth grade and earned the right to play first board on my high school chess team in my junior year."

"Learned to play the piano and often played for church services while in high school."

"Designed, constructed, and displayed a dress for a 4-H demonstration project."

"Although I was small compared to other guys, I made the first string on my high school football team."

"I graduated from high school with honors even though I was very active in school clubs and had to work part-time."

"I was the first in my family to go to college and one of the few from my high school. Worked part-time and summers. A real struggle, but I made it."

"Earned an 'A' grade on my senior psychology project from a real tough professor."

"Finished my master's degree while working full-time and attending to my family responsibilities."

"Proposed a chef's course for junior high boys. Got it approved. Developed it into a very popular elective."

"Designed the plans for our house and had it constructed within budget."

"Organized a neighborhood watch program that reduced the local crime rate by 35 percent over an initial 12-month period."

2. Prioritize your seven most significant achievements.

Your Most Significant Achievements

1. _____
2. _____
3. _____
4. _____
5. _____
6. _____
7. _____

3. Write a full page on each of your prioritized achievements. You should describe:

- How you initially became involved.
- The details of *what you did* and *how you did it.*
- What was especially enjoyable or satisfying to you.

Use copies of the "Detailing Your Achievements" form on page 83 to outline your achievements.

4. Elaborate on your achievements: Have one or two other people interview you. For each achievement have them note on a separate sheet of paper any terms used to reveal your skills, abilities, and personal qualities. To elaborate details, the interviewer(s) may ask:

- What was involved in the achievement?
- What was your part?
- What did you actually do?
- How did you go about that?

Clarify any vague areas by providing an example or illustration of what you actually did. Probe with the following questions:

Detailing Your Achievements

ACHIEVEMENT # ___: _____

_____

_____

1. How did I initially become involved? _____

    _____

    _____

    _____

2. What did I do? _____

    _____

    _____

    _____

    _____

3. How did I do it? _____

    _____

    _____

    _____

    _____

4. What was especially enjoyable about doing it?

    _____

    _____

    _____

    _____

- Would you elaborate on one example of what you mean?
- Could you give me an illustration?
- What were you good at doing?

This interview should clarify the details of your activities by asking only "what" and "how" questions. It should take 45 to 90 minutes. Make copies of the "Strength Identification Interview" form on page 85 to guide you through this interview.

5. **Identify patterns by examining the interviewer's notes:** Together identify the recurring skills, abilities, and personal qualities *demonstrated* in your achievements. Search for patterns. Your skills pattern should be clear at this point; you should feel comfortable with it. If you have questions, review the data. If you disagree with a conclusion, disregard it. The results must accurately and honestly reflect how you operate.

6. **Synthesize the information by clustering similar skills into categories:** For example, your skills might be grouped in the following manner:

Synthesized Skill Clusters

Investigate/Survey/Read Inquire/Probe/Question	Teach/Train/Drill Perform/Show/Demonstrate
Learn/Memorize/Practice Evaluate/Appraise/Assess Compare	Construct/Assemble/Put together
	Organize/Structure/Provide definition/ Plan/Chart course/Strategize/Coordinate
Influence/Involve/Get participation/Publicize/ Promote	Create/Design/Adapt/Modify

This exercise yields a relatively comprehensive inventory of your skills. The information will better enable you to use a **skills vocabulary** when identifying your objective, writing your resume and letters, and interviewing. Your self-confidence and self-esteem should increase accordingly!

Strength Identification Interview

Interviewee _____   Interviewer _____

INSTRUCTIONS: For each achievement experience, identify the **skills** and **abilities** the achiever actually demonstrated. Obtain details of the experience by asking *what* was involved with the achievement and *how* the individual made the achievement happen. Avoid "why" questions which tend to mislead. Ask for examples or illustrations of what and how.

Achievement #1:

Achievement #2:

Achievement #3:

_____

Recurring abilities and skills:

More Self-Assessment Techniques

Several other self-assessment techniques also can help you identify your motivated abilities and skills:

1. List all of your hobbies and analyze what you do in each, which ones you like the most, what skills you use, and your accomplishments.

2. Conduct a job analysis by writing about your past jobs and identifying which skills you used in each job. Cluster the skills into related categories and prioritize them according to your preferences.

3. Acquire a copy of Arthur F. Miller and Ralph T. Mattson's *The Truth About You* and work through the exercises found in the Appendix. While its overt religious message (a common theme with career counselors who enter this field with pastoral backgrounds), extreme deterministic approach, and laborious exercises may turn off some non-believers, you may find this book useful nonetheless. This is an abbreviated version of the SIMA (System for Identifying Motivated Abilities) technique used by People Management, Inc. (www.peoplemanagement.org), which is consistent with the MAS approach outlined in this chapter and is based on the work of Dr. Bernard Haldane.

4. Complete John Holland's *"The Self-Directed Search (SDS)."* You'll find it in his book, *Making Vocational Choices* or in a separate publication entitled *The Self-Directed Search – A Guide to Educational and Vocational Planning.* Also, visit the publisher's (Psychological Assessment Resources) website for an online version of the SDS: self-directed-search.com.

Computerized Assessment Systems

While the previous self-directed exercises required you to either respond to checklists of skills or reconstruct and analyze your past job experiences, several computerized self-assessment programs also help individuals identify their skills. Many of the programs are available in schools, colleges, and libraries. Some of the most widely used programs include:

- *Career Navigator*
- *Choices*
- *Discover II*
- *Guidance Information System* (GIS)
- *Self-Directed Search (SDS) Form R*
- *SIGI-Plus* (System of Interactive Guidance and Information)

Most of these computerized programs also integrate other key components in the career planning process – interests, goals, related jobs, college majors, education and training programs, and job search plans. These programs are widely available in schools, colleges, and libraries across the country. You might check with the career or counseling center at your local community college to see what computerized career assessment systems are available for your use. Relatively easy to use, they generate a great deal of useful career planning information. Many will print out a useful analysis of how your interests and skills are related to specific jobs and careers.

The New World of Online Assessment

Within the past few years, several companies have developed online assessment devices which you can quickly access via the Internet 24 hours a day in the comfort of your home or office. Some tests are self-scoring and free of charge while others require interacting with a fee-based certified career counselor or testing expert. SkillsOne (skillsone.com), for example, is operated by the producers of the *Myers-Briggs Type Indicator®* and *Strong Interest Inventory®* – Consulting Psychologists Press. CareerLab (careerlab.com) offers one of the largest batteries of well respected assessment tools: *Campbell Interest and Skills Survey, Strong Interest Inventory®, Myers-Briggs Type Indicator®, 16-Personality Factors Profile, FIRO-B, California Psychological Inventory (CPI), The Birkman Method*, and *Campbell Leadership Index.* The following seven websites are well worth exploring for both free and fee-based online assessments tools:

- SkillsOne   skillsone.com
  (Consulting Psychologists Press   cpp-db.com
- CareerLab.com   careerlab.com
- Self-Directed Search®   self-directed-search.com
- Personality Online   personalityonline.com
- Keirsey Character Sorter   keirsey.com
- MAPP™   assessment.com

These 18 additional sites also include a wealth of related assessment devices that you can access online:

- Analyze My Career   analyzemycareer.com
- Birkman Method   birkman.com
- Career Key   careerkey.org/english
- CareerLeader™   www.careerleader.com
- CareerPlanner.com   careerplanner.com
- CareerPerfect.com   careerperfect.com
- Careers By Design®   careers-by-design.com
- College Board   myroad.com
- Emode   www.emode.com
- Enneagram   ennea.com
- Humanmetrics   humanmetrics.com
- Jackson Vocational
  Interest Inventory   jvis.com
- My Future   myfuture.com
- People Management
  International   peoplemanagement.org
- Profiler   profiler.com
- QueenDom   queendom.com
- Tests on the Web   2h.com
- Tickle   web.tickle.com/tests/career.jsp

Get It Right From the Very Start

Identifying your motivated abilities and skills is one of the very first things you should do in your job search – before writing your resume, conducting research, networking, and responding to job opportunities. It is one of the best ways to prepare for telling your unique story. Once you know your major interests, skills, and abilities that motivate you to excel, you should be able to formulate a powerful employer-oriented objective and reveal in your resume and letters as well as during the interview exactly what it is you can do for the employer based upon your past pattern of performance as evidenced in your many supporting achievements. As noted in our job search diagram in Chapter 4 (page 52), self-assessment is the foundation for everything else you do in the job search. Disregard this foundation and you may sabotage your job search.

The sooner you discover what it is you do well and enjoy doing, the more focused, energetic, fun, and fascinating will be your job search. You'll approach the job world and connect with the right people from a whole new and positive perspective. You'll be able to clearly communicate to employers what it is you will most likely do for them because you have documented your accomplishments through self-assessment. Unlike other job seekers who make the mistake of not knowing their abilities and skills, and thereby have difficulty specifying an objective, you should stand out from the crowd because of your employer-centered approach. Employers will immediately know what you can do for them. Better still, they will want to invite you to an interview to learn more about your accomplishments in reference to their needs. At the interview, you will have an important story to share with them about who you are and what you will most likely do for them.

When an employer says *"You're hired!"* it's probably because you convinced them that you had the right combination of motivated abilities and skills to do the job. You had a clear behavioral advantage, because you had with the right MAS to solve their problems!

8

Neglect to Deal With Key Employment Barriers

ARE THERE CERTAIN THINGS in your background that could prevent you from getting a job? Do you lack particular attitudes, knowledge, skills, and abilities that are essential to doing the job? Do you have red flags on your resume or that pop up during the job interview that could turn off potential employers? Are you prepared to handle any objections an employer may have to hiring you?

127 Possible Barriers to Employment

Barriers to employment are roadblocks on the highway to life. They can prevent you from getting a job you want, keeping a job, or being promoted from the job you have. The potential barriers to finding and keeping a job are numerous, and may be created by many factors. Some barriers may result from behaviors that you have total control over, such as your attitudes and work habits. Other barriers may arise from circumstances you find yourself in, such as living in an area with few job opportunities or where jobs are quickly disappearing because of out-sourcing and economic downturns.

Whether the roadblocks you face result from actions within your control, or result from something seemingly beyond your control, such as where you were born and happen to live, most barriers do not have to be permanent.

Most job seekers face some combination of barriers to employment. While some barriers may be external – discrimination based on race, class, gender, age, or disability – most barriers are self-imposed due to attitudes or the lack of knowledge, skills, abilities, or willingness to take action. Survey the following checklist of 127 barriers to employment to see which ones pertain to you and require corrective action on your part:

Skills and Work History as Barriers

1 Lack adequate, or appropriate, education
2 Lack sufficient work experience
3 Lack basic reading, writing, and math skills
4 Use poor grammar
5 Use inappropriate language for the workplace
6 Lack workplace skills
7 Lack a work record – have never had a job
8 Lack a positive (good) work report – been fired
9 Lack a positive (good) work record – poor recommendation
   from former employer(s)
10 Lack a positive (good) work record – have been
    a "job hopper"
11 Have more education, training, and/or experience than
    the position requires (over qualified)
12 Lack technology skills (not technologically savvy)

Attitudes and Behaviors as Barriers

13 Engage in self-destructive behaviors – drug abuse
14 Engage in self-destructive behaviors – alcohol abuse
15 Engage in self-destructive behaviors – excessive gambling
16 Steal from employer or others
17 Make excuses rather than take responsibility
18 Speak negatively about others
19 Gossip about others

20 Appear self-centered rather than employer-centered
21 Brag about yourself
22 Exhibit a temper and express anger
23 Express intolerance of others
24 Lack initiative and self-motivation
25 Lack dependability and trustworthiness
26 Exhibit negative attitudes and character
27 Rude, disrespectful, and inconsiderate
28 Shy and introverted
29 Unwilling to learn and change behavior
30 Lack of energy and enthusiasm
31 Lack clear focus
32 Lack goals and a sense of purpose
33 Lack flexibility
34 Lack sense of entrepreneurism
35 Appear lazy
36 Tactless and insensitive
37 Wear body art that sends negative messages
38 Project a negative image
39 Lack good interpersonal skills

Health, Wellness, and Disabilities as Barriers

40 Have learning disabilities
41 Have difficult mental health issues
42 Appear overweight and unhealthy
43 Smoke or use other addictive tobacco products
44 Lack cleanliness and good personal hygiene habits
45 Appear haggard – too tired or in too poor health
    to do the work
46 Have an obvious physical disability
47 Have a history of chronic illness

Barriers to Conducting an Effective Job Search

48 Believe the job search process won't take long
49 Think you can hide or embellish your past
    through deception
50 Organize an ineffective and outdated job search

51 Lack the financial wherewithal to sustain a
   lengthy job search
52 Heavily indebted
53 Lack proper documentation
54 Look for jobs in the wrong places
55 Approach the job search for negative reasons
56 Hang around the wrong people
57 Fail to come to terms with a termination
58 Quit your job before being offered another job
59 Lack Internet access and online job search skills
60 Rely too much on the Internet
61 Have personal issues that could interfere with your work
62 Fail to do adequate research on jobs and employers
63 Appear desperate for a job
64 Primarily focus on salary and benefits
65 Try to fool employers
66 Reveal a criminal history
67 Lack adequate or reliable transportation
68 Lack a stable address or permanent housing
69 Engage in wishful thinking
70 Don't know what you want to do
71 Believe you're worth a lot more than your current pay
72 Afraid to make a job or career change
73 Apply for jobs unrelated to your qualifications
74 Show a history of job hopping
75 Unable to pass employment screening tests
76 Unlikely to get a positive background check
77 Reveal a history of on-the-job injuries and Workers'
   Compensation claims
78 Running a business while looking for a job
79 Fail to network for information, advice, and referrals
80 Use the wrong networking approach
81 Unwilling to take the necessary actions
82 Fail to properly complete applications
83 Don't write and send different types of powerful
   job search letters
84 Make numerous resume errors
85 Make numerous letter errors

 86 Send resumes and letters to the wrong places
 87 Include the wrong information or exclude important information
 88 Use the same resume and letters for different employers
 89 Fail to tell your story
 90 Fail to follow up resumes and letters
 91 Unprepared for a telephone screening interview
 92 Sound dreadful over the telephone
 93 Use negative terms
 94 Fail to mend broken fences with previous employers
 95 Violate e-mail etiquette and writing rules
 96 Fail to respond properly to job postings
 97 Arrive late for the job interview
 98 Bring a friend or relative to the job interview
 99 Project a poor image
100 Fail to engage in productive small talk
101 Unable to talk intelligently about yourself in reference to the employer's needs
102 Talk excessively rather than engage the employer
103 Lack a good command of the English language
104 Exhibit irritating and disgusting habits
105 Show little interest in the job or employer
106 Fear rejection
107 Become discouraged and depressed
108 Lie about your past
109 Exaggerate your performance
110 Attend job fairs unprepared
111 Commit one or more of 37 interview sins
112 Prematurely talk about salary and benefits
113 Reveal a great deal of personal information
114 Fail to listen carefully and respond appropriately
115 Fail to ask questions
116 Unable to give examples of your achievements
117 Fail to close the job interview properly
118 Fail to follow up interviews
119 Show a poverty of ideas and initiative
120 Fail to organize your references properly
121 Try to conduct a job search on your own

122　Look for a job involving a long commute
123　Fail to involve your spouse or significant other
　　　in your decisions
124　Take the first job offered
125　Take the first salary offered
126　Fail to get the job offer in writing
127　Forget to send thank-you letters to key people

Details on all of these barriers, as well as advice on how to deal with each, can be found in our companion volume, *Overcoming Barriers to Employment: 127 Great Tips for Putting Red Flags Behind You*. We also identify an additional 101 barriers in *Overcoming 101 More Barriers to Employment: Great Tips for Making a Habit of Career Success*.

Handling Your Red Flags

Red flags are signs that alert employers to potential problems with your candidacy. They are barriers to employment since they raise questions about your ability to do the work, fit into the workplace, or remain productive. Both your verbal and nonverbal behaviors in the job interview may raise red flags. Something you put on your resume or information omitted from your resume or application may also raise red flags in the employer's mind. Even how you follow up a job interview or negotiate a job offer may raise red flags.

Let's look at a few examples of red flags in the job search to better understand the importance of recognizing and remedying various barriers to employment. Imagine that you present the following resume to an employer. It briefly outlines six different jobs and employers in the past four years. This says to the interviewer, who looks for patterns and potential red flags, that you are a serial job hopper – experienced in sending out resumes and interviewing for jobs, you tap dance from one job to another. You either don't or can't hold a job for very long. If this employer hires you, you probably won't stay around for very long either. That means you're likely to leave or the employer will have to fire you after a few weeks or months on the job, and the employer will be left with a vacancy to fill and the need to train yet another person for the job. That costs the employer time and money. A big red flag!

Maybe it's not something you put on your resume, but something you left off. You have apparent gaps in your employment history. There are significant periods of time for which you have not indicated what you were doing. The employer is left to wonder what you are hiding. You must be hiding something, or you would have indicated on your resume what you were doing for the time period. A big red flag. Or you arrive late for your job interview. Lots of red flags are waving in front of the interviewer's eyes. If you can't even be on time for the job interview, how can an employer expect you'll be on time for work every day?

> *Red flags are barriers to employment since they raise questions about your ability to do the work, fit into the workplace, or remain productive.*

If you recognize yourself in any of these scenarios, you have potholes in your life. Each of the potholes is a barrier. The red flags simply alert the employer to the existence of the potholes. To overcome the barriers that get in the way of your employment, you must first recognize the pothole (barrier), and the reason this is a concern to an employer (red flag), and then repair the pothole to remove the barrier and smooth out the highway.

Useful Resources

These resources (available at www.impactpublications.com) address numerous barriers to employment and how to best overcome them:

95 Mistakes Job Seekers Make and How to Avoid Them
Job Hunting Tips for People With Hot and Not-So-Hot
*   Backgrounds*
Job Interview Tips for People With Not-So-Hot Backgrounds
No One Is Unemployable
Overcoming Barriers to Employment
Overcoming 101 More Barriers to Employment
Resume, Applications, and Letter Tips for People With Hot and
*   Not-So-Hot Backgrounds*
Winning Letters That Overcome Barriers to Employment

9

Write and Distribute Awful Resumes and Letters

E VERYONE, INCLUDING EMPLOYERS, seems to have a love-hate relationship with resumes and letters. While we know these documents are important to the job search and recruitment processes, few people are really satisfied with the form and content of this written communication. Some people even go so far as to advise against writing resumes and letters. As a result, we always seem to be giving advice on how to make resumes and letters more effective, from writing each section to distributing them by mail, fax, or email. With so much written about resumes and letters, one might think there was something very magical about them. Maybe they get jobs?

Another Rogue's Gallery of Errors

One of the very top job search problems is this: Many job seekers write awful resumes and letters that work against their best interests. Their resumes and letters are frequently "dead upon arrival" because of many common writing, production, and distribution errors. If they're not dead upon arrival, they often go nowhere because of the failure to follow up. Worst of all, most job seekers are unaware how bad their resumes and letters may be in the eyes of employers. Intensely ego-involved with the writing process, like an admiring photo of themselves, most job seekers like their resumes and letters. They just don't understand why employers don't like them as much as they do!

Misunderstanding Resumes, and Letters

The most important error job seekers make in reference to resumes and letters is misunderstanding the role these documents play in the overall job search. They mistakenly believe that resumes and letters result in jobs. They don't. Accordingly, they try to put as much information as possible about their work history on their resume. Many can't understand how they could possibly get everything about themselves onto one or two pages – the preferred length of resumes for employers.

Your resume should give just enough information to motivate the reader to invite you to an interview.

If there is only one thing you learn about resumes and letters that will serve you well throughout your job search, it's this: Resumes and letters are advertisements for interviews. Like a good ad in a magazine, they should give just enough information to motivate the reader to acquire the product. That product is you being invited to an interview. Always remember that it's the job interview – not a resume or letter – that results in a job offer. If you define resumes and letters as advertising mediums rather than summaries of one's history, you'll be surprised how many resume and letter mistakes you'll automatically avoid. You'll easily be able to produce a one- to two-page advertisement about what benefits you are likely to give the reader, and you'll be very careful of the choice of words you use and you'll pay particular attention to making sure you produce picture-perfect and error-free copy.

Deadly Myths and Promising Realities

Numerous myths surround resumes and letters. Misunderstanding what these written documents are all about prevents many job seekers from taking effective action. Over the years we have catalogued nearly 30 myths and corresponding realities for clarifying the use of resumes and letters in an effective job search. Each myth and reality relates to various aspects of writing, producing, distributing, and following up resumes and letters:

Winning the Job

MYTH 1:   **The best way to find a job is to respond to classified ads, use employment agencies, submit applications, and send resumes and cover letters to personnel offices and online databases.**

REALITY: While many people get jobs by following such formal application procedures, these are not the most effective ways to get the best jobs – those offering good pay, advancement opportunities, and an appropriate "fit" with one's abilities and goals. Most of the best jobs are neither listed nor advertised; they are primarily uncovered through word-of-mouth and executive recruiters or by knocking on doors. Your most fruitful job search strategy will be to network for information, advice, and referrals in the "hidden job market."

MYTH 2:   **A good resume and cover letter will get me a job.**

REALITY: Resumes and letters don't get jobs – they advertise you for interviews. Your resumes and letters are **marketing tools** designed to communicate your qualifications to employers. From the perspective of employers, resumes and letters are used to screen candidates – who are basically strangers to employers – for interviews.

MYTH 3:   **The candidate with the best education, skills, and experience will get the job.**

REALITY: Employers hire individuals for many different reasons. Education, skills, and experience are only a few of the various hiring criteria. Surprising to some candidates, these criteria may **not** be the most important in the eyes of many employers. Employers interview candidates because they want to see warm bodies – how you look and interact with them and how you will fit into their organization. The most important reason for hiring you is that the employer "likes" you. How "likes" is defined will vary from one employer and organization to another.

MYTH 4:   **You can plan all you want, but getting a job is really a function of good luck.**

REALITY: Luck is a function of being in the right place at the right time to take advantage of opportunities that come your way. But how do you plan your luck? The best way to have luck come your way is to plan to be in many different places at many different times through networking.

Deciding on Resume Content

MYTH 5:   **The best type of resume is one that outlines employment history by job titles, responsibilities, and inclusive employment dates.**

REALITY: This is the traditional chronological or "obituary" resume. It's filled with historical "what" information – what work you did, in what organizations, over what period of time. This type of resume may tell employers little about what it is you can do for them. You should choose a resume format that clearly co mmunicates yo ur m ajor strengths. Yo ur choices include variations of the chronological, functional, and combination resumes – each offering different advantages and disadvantages.

MYTH 6:   **It's not necessary to put an objective on the resume.**

REALITY: Survey research (The McLean Group and the Career Masters Institute, February 2002) with employers validates the importance of objectives on resumes: employers are especially attracted to resumes that include objectives that either state an applicant's career goal (what he or she wants to do career-wise) or what an applicant can do for the organization. Employers are especially attracted to coherent resumes that are easy to read and interpret. An objective – stated at the very top of your resume – becomes the central focus from which all other elements on your resume should flow. The objective gives the resume organization, coherence, and direction. It tells employers exactly who you are in terms of your goals and skills. If properly stated, your objective will become one of the most powerful and effective statements on your resume. Without an objective, you force the employer to "interpret" your resume. Thus, it is to your advantage to set the agenda – control the flow and interpretation of your qualifications and capabilities by stating the objective. If nothing else, stating an objective on your resume is a thoughtful thing to do for the employer. And always remember, employers "like" thoughtful people!

MYTH 7:   **Employers prefer long resumes because they present more complete information for screening candidates than short resumes.**

REALITY: Employers prefer one- or two-page resumes. Longer resumes lose the interest and attention of readers. They usually lack a focus, are filled with extraneous information, need editing, and are oriented toward the applicant's past rather than the employer's future. But this one- to two-page rule does not apply to all employment situations. Individuals applying for academic and international jobs, for example, may be expected to write a five- to 10-page curriculum vitae (CV) rather than a one- to two-page resume. In these special situations the CV is actually a traditional chronological resume prominently displaying dates, job titles, responsibilities, and publications.

MYTH 8:   **It's okay to put salary expectations on a resume.**

REALITY: One of the worst things you can do is to mention salary on your resume. Remember, the purpose of your resume is to get an interview. Only during the interview – and preferably toward the end – should you discuss salary. And before you discuss salary, you want to demonstrate your **value** to employers as well as learn about the **worth** of the position.

MYTH 9: **Contact information (name, address, phone number, email) should appear in the left-hand corner of your resume.**

REALITY: You can choose from a variety of resume formats which place the contact information in several different positions at the top of the resume. Choose the one that best complements the remaining layout and style of the resume.

MYTH 10: **You should not include your hobbies or any personal statements on a resume.**

REALITY: In general this is true. However, there are exceptions which would challenge this rule as a myth. If you have a hobby or a personal statement that can strengthen your objective in relation to the employer's needs, do include it on your resume. For example, if a job calls for someone who is outgoing and energetic, you would not want to include a hobby or personal statement that indicates that you are a very private and sedentary person, such as *"enjoy reading and writing"* or *"collect stamps."* But *"enjoy organizing community fund drives"* and *"co mpete in the Boston Marathon"* might be very appropriate statements for your resume. Such statements further emphasize the "unique you" in relation to your capabilities, the requirements for the position, and the employer's needs.

MYTH 11: **You should list your references on the resume so the employer can check them before the interview.**

REALITY: Never include references on your resume. The closest you should ever get to doing so is to include this statement at the very end: "References available upon request." **You** want to control your references for the interview.

Producing the Resume

MYTH 12: **You should try to get as much as possible on each page of your resume.**

REALITY: Each page of your resume should be appealing to the eye. It should make an immediate favorable impression, be inviting and easy to read, and lo ok professional. You achieve these qualities by using a variety of layout, type style, highlighting, and emphasizing techniques. When formatting each section of your resume, be sure to make generous use of white space. Bullet and underline items for emphasis. If you try to cram a great deal on each page, your resume will look cluttered and uninviting to the reader.

MYTH 13: **You should have your resume produced by a graphic designer and professionally printed.**

REALITY: You may want to go to the expense of hiring a graphic designer and printing, depending on your audience. However, it is not necessary for most positions to go to such an extreme in order to impress your reader. Just make sure your resume looks first-class and professional. Employers are more interested in the content of your resume – documented work history, accomplishments, education, and objective related to their specific hiring needs – than in the "dress for success" visual elements.

MYTH 14: **The weight and color of the resume's paper and ink are unimportant to employers.**

REALTY: Weight, paper color, and ink do count, but how much they count in comparison to resume content is difficult to say. These are the very first things the employer sees and feels when receiving your resume. They make an important initial impression. If your resume doesn't look and feel right during the first five seconds, the reader may not feel good about reading the contents of your resume. Make a good initial impression by selecting a good weight and color of paper. Your resume should have a substantive feel to the touch – use nothing less than 20-pound paper which also has some texture. But don't go to extremes with a very heavy and roughly textured paper. Stay with conservative paper colors: white, off-white, ivory, light tan, or light grey.

MYTH 15:   **You should make at least 100 copies of your resume.**

REALITY: Make only as many as you need – which may be only one. If you word-process your resume, you can customize each resume for each position for which you apply. Your production needs should be largely determined by your strategy for distributing your resume.

Writing Job Search Letters

MYTH 16:   **It's okay to send your resume to an employer without an accompanying cover letter.**

REALITY: Only if you want the employer to think his or her position and employment opportunity are not important. Sending a resume without a cover letter is like going to a job interview barefoot – your application is incomplete and your resume is not being properly communicated for action. Cover letters should always accompany resumes that are sent through the mail.

MYTH 17:   **The purpose of a cover letter is to introduce your resume to an employer.**

REALITY: A cover letter should be much more than mere cover for a resume. If written properly, a cover letter enables you to express important qualities sought by employers in the job interview – your personality, style, energy, and enthusiasm. Like good advertising copy, your cover letter should be the "sizzle" or headline accompanying your resume. After all, the purpose of a cover letter should be to get the employer to **take action** on your resume. Consequently, the whole structure of your cover letter should focus on persuading the employer to invite you for a job interview.

MYTH 18: End your letter indicating that you expect to hear from the employer: *"I look forward to hearing from you."*

REALITY: What do you expect will happen when you close your letter in this manner? Probably nothing. You want specific **action** to result from your written communication. Any type of action – positive or negative – should help you move on to the next stage of your job search with this or other potential employers. It's best to close your letter with an action statement like this one:

> *I'll give you a call Thursday afternoon to answer any questions you may have regarding my interests and qualifications.*

Such a statement, in effect, invites you to a telephone interview – the first step to getting a face-to-face job interview. While some employers may avoid your telephone call, at least you will get some action in reference to your letter and resume.

MYTH 19: The cover letter should attempt to sell the employer on your qualifications.

REALITY: The cover letter should command attention and nicely provide a cover for an enclosure – your resume. This letter should be professional, polite, personable, and to the point. Avoid repeating in this letter what's on your resume.

MYTH 20: Handwritten cover letters have a greater impact on employers than typed cover letters.

REALITY: Handwritten cover letters are inappropriate, as are scribbled notes on or attached to a resume. They are **too** personal and look unprofessional when applying for a job. You want to demonstrate that you can present yourself to others in the most professional manner possible. Confine your handwriting activities to your signature only.

MYTH 21:   **Letters are not very important in a job search. The only letter you need to write is a formal cover letter.**

REALITY: Your letters actually may be more important than your resume. In fact, cover letters are only one of several types of letters you should write during your job search:

- Resume letters
- Approach letters
- Thank-you letters

Different types of thank-you letters should be written on various job search occasions:

- Post-job interview
- After informational interview
- Responding to a rejection
- Withdrawing from consideration
- Accepting job offer
- Terminating employment

These are some of the most neglected yet most important forms of written communications in any job search. If you write these letters, your job search may take you much further than you expected!

Distributing Resumes and Letters

MYTH 22:   **It is best to send out numerous resumes and letters to prospective employers in the hope that a few will invite you to an interview.**

REALITY: Yes, if you play the odds, someone might call you. In fact, if you broadcast resumes and letters to 1,000 employers, you may have two or three invite you to an interview. However, this approach is more appropriate for people who are in desperate need of a job or who don't know what they want to do. Some inexpensive executive resume email blasting services ($19.95 to email a resume to 10,000 ostensibly interested parties – see resumeblaster.com, blast myresume.com, executiveagent.com), which primarily email resumes to headhunters, claim remarkable results. This non-focused approach will initially give you a false sense of making progress with your job search. You should concentrate on targeting your resume on particular organizations, employers, and positions that most interest you. This approach will require you to network for information and job leads. As such, you will seldom send a resume and cover letter through the mail or by email.

MYTH 23: **You should present your resume at the beginning of an informational interview.**

REALITY: Never ever introduce yourself with your resume. Instead, your resume should be presented at the very **end** of the informational interview. Keep in mind that the purpose of an informational interview is to get information, advice, and referrals. You are not asking for a job. If you present your resume at the beginning of such an interview, you give the impression that you are looking for a job. Near the end of the interview you want to ask the interviewer to review your resume and give you advice on how to strengthen it and suggest where you might send it.

Following Up

MYTH 24: **Once you distribute your resume and letters, there is little you can do other than wait to be called for an interview.**

REALITY: If you do nothing, you are likely to get nothing. There are many things you can do. First, you can write more letters to inquire about your application status. Second, you can telephone the employer for more information on when the interview and hiring decisions will take place. Third, you can telephone to request an interview at a convenient time. The first approach will likely result in no response. The second approach will probably give you an inconclusive answer. The third approach will give you a *"yes"* or *"no."* We prefer the third approach.

MYTH 25:   **The best way to follow up on your application and resume is to write a letter of inquiry.**

REALITY: Employers are busy people who do not have time to read all their email and snail mail, much less sit down to write letters. Use the telephone instead. It's much more efficient and effective. Be sure to keep good records of all correspondence, telephone conversations, and meetings. Keep a paper or electronic file on each prospective employer.

Using New Types of Resumes

MYTH 26:   **Electronic resumes are the wave of the future. You must write and distribute them to get a good job.**

REALITY: During the past 10 years electronic resumes (scannable, emailable, HTML, video, and multimedia) have played an important role in the job search and recruitment processes. However, numerous changes have taken place during the past few years due to rapid advances in resume screening and processing technology. For example, scannable resumes have become obsolete. Ugly duckling ASCII resumes are disappearing as employers increasingly receive formatted resumes via the Internet. Many employers now require applicants to complete an online form that produces a "profile" in lieu of a regular resume. At present no one electronic resume fits all employers. Electronic resumes are structured around "keywords" or nouns which stress capabilities. While such resumes may be excellent candidates for searchable resume databases and online applicant systems, they may be weak documents for human readers. Since human beings interview and hire, you should first create a resume that follows the principles of human communication. For now, we also recommend developing a separate resume designed for email transmission. We're less enthusiastic about HTML, video, and multimedia resumes. For an update on the changing technology of employers for receiving, screening, and processing resumes, see Joyce Lain Kennedy's fourth edition of *Resumes for Dummies* (John Wiley & Sons), in which she focuses on the return of the "beautiful resume" with the new technology. The fifth edition of this book, which comes off press in January 2007, will further update changes in electronic resumes. At the same time, keep in mind that the resume requirements differ given the size of the company. A company with 50,000 employees will most likely be on the technological cutting edge for receiving, screening, and processing electronic resumes than a company with only 10 employees which may still accept mailed and faxed resumes. Most employers, regardless of the size of their companies, now prefer to receive resumes by email.

MYTH 27:   **Individuals who include their resumes in resume banks or post them online in resume databases are more likely to get high paying jobs than those that don't.**

REALITY: During the past 10 years most electronic resume banks have become victims of the "free" Internet. They have either gone out of business or have transformed their operations by becoming resume databases on the Internet. While some resume banks and databases still charge users monthly or yearly membership fees, most are now supported by employers who advertise on the sites and/or pay fees to access resumes online through particular Internet employment sites. Essentially a high-tech approach for broadcasting resumes, inclusion of your resume in these resume banks and databases means your resume literally works 24 hours a day. Major employers increasingly use these resume banks and databases for locating qualified candidates, especially for screening individuals with technical skills. And we know some individuals who join these resume banks do get jobs. However, there is no evidence that most people belonging to these groups ever get interviews or jobs through such membership. Nor is there any evidence that membership results in higher paying jobs than nonmembership. The real advantage of such groups is this: they open new channels for contacting employers whom you might not otherwise come into contact with. Indeed, some employers only use these resume banks and databases for locating certain types of candidates rather than use more traditional channels, such as newspapers and employment offices, for advertising positions and recruiting candidates. Employers find the Internet to be a much cheaper way of recruiting personnel than through the more traditional approach of purchasing classified ads or hiring employment firms or headhunters.

MYTH 28: **The video resume is the wave of the future. You need to develop a video resume and send it to prospective employers.**

REALITY: The video resume is a novel approach to the employment process. However, since it is video-based, it's really a misnomer to call these videos a form of "resume." The so-called video resume functions more as a screening interview than a resume. Remember, the purpose of a resume is to get an interview. A video includes key elements that are best presented in a face-to-face interview – verbal and nonverbal communication. Unless requested by an employer in lieu of a traditional resume, we recommend avoiding the use of the video resume. However, if you are applying for a position that requires good presentation skills best demonstrated in the video format, such as in sales, broadcasting, and entertainment, the video resume may be the perfect approach to employers. But make sure you do a first-class job in developing the video. Avoid amateur products which will probably reflect badly on your skills.

MYTH 29: **You should develop your own home page on the Internet and direct employers to your site.**

REALITY: Do this only if you are a real professional and can customize your site to particular employers. Like the video resume, home pages can be double-edged swords. Some employers may like them, but others may dislike them. Your particular site may reflect poorly on your qualifications, especially if it is not designed like a resume, i.e., stresses your accomplishments and goals. Furthermore, since most employers are too busy trying to get through paper resumes and letters, few have the time or desire to access your Internet site, unless your paper resume and letter sufficiently motivate them to do so. Like viewing videos, accessing sites on the Internet takes time. Remember, employers can still screen a paper resume and letter within 30 seconds! Why would they want to spend 15 minutes trying to access and review yo ur site when they could be dispensing with another 30 resumes and letters during that time? If you decide to go this route, you'll need to give employers a good reason why they should invest such time looking for you on the Internet!

Resume Writing Mistakes

Many resumes are literally "dead upon arrival" because the job seeker made serious writing errors. Employers frequently report the following common mistakes resume writers make which often eliminate them from competition. Most of these mistakes center on issues of focus, organization, trustworthiness, intelligence, and competence. Reading between the lines, employers often draw conclusions about the individual's personality and competence based upon the number of errors found on the resume. If you make any of these errors, chances are your **credibility** will be called into question. Make sure your resume does not commit any of these writing errors:

1. Unrelated to the position in question.
2. Too long or too short.
3. Unattractive with a poorly designed format, small type style, and crowded copy.
4. Misspellings, poor grammar, wordiness, and redundancy.
5. Punctuation errors.
6. Lengthy phrases, long sentences, and awkward paragraphs.

7. Slick, amateurish, or "gimmicky" – appears over-produced.
8. Boastful, egocentric, and aggressive.
9. Dishonest, untrustworthy, or suspicious information.
10. Missing critical categories, such as experience, skills, and education.
11. Difficult to interpret because of poor organization and lack of focus; uncertain what the person has done or can do.
12. Unexplained time gaps between jobs.
13. Too many jobs in a short period of time – a job hopper with little evidence of career advancement.
14. No evidence of past accomplishments or a pattern of performance from which to predict future performance. Primarily focuses on formal duties and responsibilities that came with previous jobs.
15. Lacks credibility and content – includes much fluff and "canned" resume language.
16. States a strange, unclear, or vague objective.
17. Appears over-qualified or under-qualified for the position.
18. Includes distracting personal information that does not enhance the resume nor candidacy.
19. Fails to include critical contact information (telephone number and email address) and uses an anonymous address (P.O. Box number).
20. Uses jargon and abbreviations unfamiliar to the reader.
21. Embellishes name with formal titles, middle names, and nicknames which make him or her appear odd or strange.
22. Repeatedly refers to "I" and appears self-centered.
23. Includes obvious self-serving references that raise credibility questions.
24. Sloppy, with handwritten corrections – crosses out "married" and writes "single"!
25. Includes "red flag" information such as being fired, lawsuits or claims, health or performance problems, or starting salary figures, including salary requirements that may be too high or too low.

Production, Distribution, and Follow-Up Errors

Assuming you have written a great resume and a very persuasive cover letter, your next challenge is to make sure you don't make several errors relating to the production, distribution, and follow-up stages of your resumes and letters. Here are some of the most common such errors you must avoid:

1. Poorly typed and reproduced – hard to read.
2. Produced on odd-sized paper.
3. Printed on poor quality paper or on extremely thin or thick paper.
4. Soiled with coffee stains, fingerprints, or ink marks.
5. Sent to the wrong person or department.
6. Mailed, faxed, or emailed to "To Whom It May Concern" or "Dear Sir."
7. Emailed as an attachment which could have a virus if opened.
8. Enclosed in a tiny envelope that requires the resume to be unfolded and flattened several times.
9. Arrived without proper postage – the employer gets to pay the extra!
10. Sent the resume and letter by the slowest postage rate possible.
11. Envelope double-sealed with tape and is indestructible – nearly impossible to open by conventional means!
12. Back of envelope includes a handwritten note stating that something is missing on the resume, such as a telephone number, email address, or new mailing address.
13. Resume taped to the inside of the envelope, an old European habit practiced by paranoid letter writers. Need to destroy the envelope and perhaps the resume as well to get it out.
14. Accompanied by extraneous or inappropriate enclosures which were not requested, such as copies of self-serving letters or recommendations, transcripts, or samples of work.
15. Arrives too late for consideration.
16. Comes without a cover letter.
17. Cover letter repeats what's on the resumes – does not command attention nor move the reader to action.

18. Sent the same or different versions of the resume to the same person as a seemingly clever follow-up method.
19. Follow-up call made too soon – before the resume and letter arrive!
20. Follow-up call is too aggressive or the candidate appears too "hungry" for the position – appears needy or greedy.

Whatever you do, make sure you write, produce, and distribute error-free resumes and letters. If you commit any of the errors outlined in this chapter, chances are you will be eliminated from consideration or your candidacy will be greatly diminished.

The Perfect Resume and Letter

The perfect resume and letter stress objectives, skills, and accomplishments as well as avoid the many errors committed by job seekers. While you can use many different resume and letter writing forms, the examples on pages 114-116 make excellent advertisements for job interviews. Look at them carefully. These are employer-centered documents designed to move the reader to take action – invite the candidate to a job interview. The letter example on page 117 is the classic "T-letter" – one of the most powerful job search letters you can write. This type of letter, which forms a "T" between the employer's requirements and the candidate's qualifications, can be sent along with or in lieu of a resume.

Martin Wellstone
4319 Wilson Boulevard
Tampa, Florida 16789
Tel. 789-234-9876
Email: martinw@newnet.com

Objective

A challenging position using skills in **Financial Analysis, Security Analysis, Budget Analysis,** and **Investment Strategies** that will be used to:

- strengthen a company's financial position
- identify new investment opportunities
- develop effective financial strategies
- forecast and manage future performance

Qualifications Summary

Detailed and results-oriented individual with strong analytical and entrepreneurial skills in accounting and financial systems. Adept at using statistical and other forecasting models for creating budgets, improving business operations, and developing investment strategies. Proven ability to create and implement effective cost management systems. Over 8 years of progressive responsibility and expertise in financial environments dealing with:

Financial Analysis/Planning	Investment Analysis	Accounting
Strategic Planning	Cash Management	Contracting
Credit Analysis	Budget Analysis	Valuation
Mergers and Acquisitions	Financial Management	Research
E-commerce	Risk Management	Project Management

Experience and Accomplishments

Finance

- Managed financial operation of government contractor with $15 million in assets and $25 million in annual revenue. **Results:** Saved over $50,000 in an nual accounting costs by strengthening leadership over all accounting, payroll, banking, and risk management functions.

- Analyzed financial statements and other related reports, using ratio analysis to identify possible weaknesses in the company's financial operations and recommended remedial actions. **Results:** Improved procedures enabled company to develop aggressive marketing strategy for generating an additional $5 million in revenue.

- Developed and administered new defined contribution, profit sharing, and cafeteria plans. **Results:** Employee turnover reduced by 20 percent over a 12-month period.

- Prepared reports that summarized and forecasted company business activity based on past, present, and expected operations. Used various forecasting techniques, such as regression, moving averages, and other econometric models, to establish the forecasted figures. **Results:** Earnings forecasts, which were 95 percent accurate in the first six months, established new investment strategy for achieving a 20 percent annual growth rate.

- Created the operational, cash, and capital budgets of several small companies. Introduced simplified small business accounting software programs to manage day-to-day accounting functions. **Results:** Saved each business over $30,000 annually by eliminating the need to hire a full-time accountant.

Accounting

- Defended employer before Contract Board of Appeals. **Results:** Saved employer over $200,000 in disallowed contract costs emanating from a FTAC audit.

- Performed all facets of accounting, including accounts payable, receivable, payroll functions, and general ledger account reconciliation and bank reconciliation statements. **Results:** Eliminated the need for two part-time bookkeeping positions and thus saved employer over $40,000 a year in personnel costs.

- Prepared corporate financial statements, including income statements, balance sheets, and cash flow statements for both internal and external reporting. **Results:** Improved on-time reporting by 300% within first six months and developed attractive financial portfolio for generating $8 million in outside investment.

- Introduced a budgetary system that inculcated a culture of cost control awareness. **Results:** Streamlined the service delivery system of a training company and saved over $100,000 annually in wasteful processes.

- Developed sensitivity models for determining break-even sales volume for each corporate division. **Results:** Improved profitability of five divisions by 15 percent within six months and eliminated one unprofitable division which saved the company more than $200,000.

Professional Experience

DELTA COMPUTER SERVICES, Orlando, FL   2004 – Present
Controller

THE TRAINING GROUP, Atlanta, GA   1999 – 2003
Senior Accountant

SEVEN SMALL BUSINESSES   1994 – Present
Part-time consultant in various aspects of accounting

Education

University of Illinois   MBA, Finance   2003

- Developed award-winning e-commerce business model for reaching undergraduate students
- Interned with KPMG as Investment Analyst

Vanderbilt University   BA, Accounting   1998

- Graduated with Honors, 3.8/4.0
- Worked full-time in earning 100% of educational and personal expenses

Computer Skills

- Microsoft Word   - Excel   - Access   - PowerPoint
  - InDesign   - PhotoShop   - Lotus Notes

Memberships and Affiliations

- Society of Investment Analysts   - American Society of Accountants
- American Association of Individual Investors   - Toastmasters International

July 8, 20___

Mary Christus
Silver Lake Products
873 Timberlake Drive
Phoenix, AZ 88888

Dear Ms. Christus:

I am responding to your job announcement that appeared on the HotJobs site yesterday for a Public Relations Specialist. My resume is available online (#281481) with CareerWeb and I emailed a copy to you yesterday per your instructions.

I believe I may be the perfect candidate for this position given my more than eight years of progressive, results-oriented experience in Public Relations:

Your Requirements	**My Qualifications**
5+ years of experience in PR	8+ years of experience in PR as well as sales and marketing. I understand the important relationship between PR and sales and marketing.
Strong interpersonal skills.	Consistently praised on annual performance appraisal as *"adept in working well with both co-workers and clients."* Twice received "Employee of the Year" Award.
Ability to bring in new accounts.	Maintained and significantly expanded (20% annually) client base of key accounts that generate 30% of employer's total revenue base – up from 5% when hired three years ago.
Energetic and willing to travel.	Work well with deadlines and stressful situations. Energy and enthusiasm cited by clients as a main reason for working with Joan Riley. Love to travel and do so frequently in working with clients and participating in professional activities.

In addition, I know the importance of building strong customer relations and developing innovative approaches to today's new PR mediums. I love taking on new challenges, working in multiple team and project settings, and seeing clients achieve results from my company's efforts.

I believe there is a strong match between your needs and my professional interests and qualifications. Could we meet soon to discuss how we might best work together? I'll call your office Thursday at 2pm to see if your schedule might permit such a meeting.

I appreciate your consideration and look forward to speaking with you on Thursday.

Sincerely,

Joan Riley

Joan Riley

Useful Books and Software

A disproportionate number of books focus on resumes and letters. They cover almost every occupation as well as different classes of workers – blue collar, recent graduates, and CEOs making over $100,000 a year. Most books fall into one of three categories:

1. Emphasize the process of writing each resume and letter section as well address the critical issues of production, distribution, and follow-up.

2. Present examples of excellent resumes and letters produced by professional resume writers and/or talented job seekers.

3. Focus on the special case of electronic and Internet resumes.

The majority of resume and letter books primarily present examples with very little useful process information on how to write, produce, distribute, and follow up. The following books should prove useful:

Primary Focus on Process With Examples

Cover Letters for Dummies
Haldane's Best Cover Letters for Professionals
Haldane's Best Resumes for Professionals
High Impact Resumes and Letters
Nail the Cover Letter
Nail the Resume
Power Resumes
Resumes for Dummies
Winning Letters That Overcome Barriers to Employment

Primary Focus on Presenting Examples

101 Best Resumes
175 High-Impact Cover Letters
175 High-Impact Resumes
America's Top Resumes for America's Top Jobs

Best Cover Letters for $100,000+ Jobs
Best Resumes for $100,000+ Jobs
Cover Letters That Knock 'em Dead
Expert Resumes for People Returning to Work
Gallery of Best Cover Letters
Gallery of Best Resumes
No-Nonsense Cover Letters
No-Nonsense Resumes
Resumes That Knock 'Em Dead

Special Case of Electronic and Internet Resumes

Cyberspace Resume Kit
Electronic Resumes and Online Networking
e-Resumes
Internet Resumes
Resumes in Cyberspace

Several software programs assist individuals in quickly producing resumes that follow standard computer-generated formats. Two of the most popular such programs include:

ResumeMaker
WinWay Resume Deluxe 10.0

Online Writing Assistance and Services

Several websites provide useful tips on how to write resumes and letters:

▪ Monster.com	resume.monster.com
▪ America's CareerInfoNet	www.acinet.org/acinet
▪ JobStar	jobstar.org/tools/resume
▪ CareerBuilder	careerbuilder.com
▪ Career Journal	careerjournal.com/job hunting/resumes
▪ Quintessential Careers	quintcareers.com
▪ Wetfeet	wetfeet.com
▪ WinningTheJob	www.winningthejob.com

A few sites, such as vault.com, even provide a free online resume review by a career professional. Other sites, such as careerbuilder.com ("Advice & Resources"), primarily include sponsored links to companies that offer fee-based resume writing and distribution services. Resume writing professionals, such as author Rebecca Smith, maintain their own websites (eresumes.com) with tips on writing an electronic resume.

If you feel you could benefit from the services of a professional resume writer, expect to pay between $100 to $500 for a resume, and check out these websites for assistance:

■ Professional Association of Resume Writers and Career Coaches	www.parw.com
■ Professional Resume Writing and Research Association	prwra.com
■ National Resume Writers' Association	nrwaweb.com
■ Career Masters Institute	cminstitute.com

At the same time, check out some of these websites which are sponsored by professional resume writers. Most of them will give you a free resume critique prior to using their fee-based services:

■ A&A Resume	aandaresume.com
■ A-Advanced Resume Service	topsecretresumes.com
■ Advanced Career Systems	resumesystems.com
■ Advanced Resume Services	resumeservices.com
■ The Advantage	advantageresume.com
■ Cambridge Resume Service	cambridgeresume.com
■ Career Resumes	career-resumes.com
■ CertifiedResumeWriters	certifiedresumewriters.com
■ eResume (Rebecca Smith's)	eresumes.com
■ e-resume.net	e-resume.net
■ ExecutiveAgent.com	executiveagent.com
■ Free-Resume-Tips	free-resume-tips.com
■ Impact Resumes	impactresumes.com
■ Leading Edge Resumes	leadingedgeresumes.com
■ Resume Agent	resumeagent.com

- Resume.com   resume.com
- ResumeMaker   resumemaker.com
- Resume Writer   resumewriter.com
- WSACORP.com   www.wsacorp.com

Resume Blasting Services

Resume distribution approaches have always been controversial, whether offline or online. Indeed, career counselors usually caution job seekers about literally "throwing money to the wind" by shotgunning, or blasting, their resumes to hundreds of employers. This approach usually gives job seekers a false sense of hope – they feel they are actually doing something to advance their job search by reaching out by mail or email to literally touch potential employers! However, this is usually the approach of unfocused, and often desperate and unrealistic, job seekers. As the Internet increasingly plays an important role in the job search, several companies now specialize in blasting resumes via email to hundreds individuals possibly interested in receiving such resumes. For a fee ranging from $19.95 to $199.95, they will email your resume to a special list of executive recruiters and employers, but primarily to executive recruiters. We're very dubious about this approach, despite many self-serving testimonials to the contrary. You'll probably get what you pay for using this borderline spam approach to resume distribution – little to nothing and lots of false hopes. If you're interested in trying your luck with this approach, check out these resume blasting sites which include information on their services:

- Allen and Associates   resumexpress.com
- BlastMyResume   blastmyresume.com
- CareerXpress.com   careerxpress.com
- DeliverMyResume   delivermyresume.com
- E-cv.com   e-cv.com
- Executiveagent.com   executiveagent.com
- HotResumes   hotresumes.com
- Job Search Page   jobsearchpage.com
                             (international focus)
- Job Village   jobvillage.com
- Resume Agent   resumeagent.com

- ResumeBlaster   resumeblaster.com
- Resume Booster   resumebooster.com
- ResumeBroadcaster   resumebroadcaster.com
- ResumeMachine.com   resumemachine.com
- Resume Rabbit   resumerabbit.com
                             (posts to multiple job boards)
- ResumeZapper   resumezapper.com
- ResumeXpress   resumexpress.com
- RocketResume   rocketresume.com
- See Me Resumes   seemeresumes.com
- WSACORP.com   www.wsacorp.com

Tooting Your Horn With Focus

Regardless of all the myths, mistakes, and cautionary notes about writing, producing, distributing, and following up resumes and letters, many job seekers continue to abuse this important step in their job search. Perhaps it's because there is still something very mystical about these highly ego-involved documents that also seem to violate one of mother's early childhood rules – don't talk about yourself to others! Lacking practice in tooting their horn, many job seekers appear confused about how to best present themselves on resumes and in letters. However, presenting your best self on paper should be a relatively easy task if you stay focused on what employers really look for in candidates – evidence of past, present, and future performance relevant to their needs. If you can keep this focus and remember the central purpose of resumes, you should be able to avoid most of the resume and letter sins outlined in this chapter. Your resume should grab the attention of employers, who will want to interview you for a job.

10

Mess Up the Critical Job Interview

THE JOB INTERVIEW IS THE most important step in the job search. Everything you do up to this point in your job search should be designed to get the interview. Once you get an interview, which may become a series of three or four interviews with a single employer, your goal should be to learn as much as possible about the job and employer so you can make an informed decision whether or not you want the position. As such, the interview becomes a two-way communication process – you assess the employer and the employer assesses you to decide whether or not you want to work together.

Unfortunately, many job seekers finally get the job interview and then make a series of errors that either knock them out of competition or result in making bad employment decisions. Many of the errors may seem unbelievable, but they occur every day with thousands of candidates.

Stressful Times

Congratulations! You've just been invited to a job interview. Your job search efforts, from self-assessment and research to resume writing and networking, have finally paid off. All you have to do now is go into the job interview and sell yourself. However, that's easier said than done. The very thought of going to a job interview touches on a full range of emotions – joy at getting the interview and sweaty palms thinking about what to wear, say, and do during the interview. Like an actor in the theater, you will be onstage facing a critical audience who will ask you many probing questions to determine whether or not to offer you the job. Chances are you are competing with other equally qualified candidates, which may string out the hiring decision for two to three weeks.

The job interview is one of the most stressful situations you may encounter, and especially if you really want the job in question. Within the space of a few days, you need to get ready for a major performance. Perhaps you should rehearse a few lines about why you are the perfect fit for this job. But the interview is more than just talk centering on a series of questions and answers. It's also about making a good impression, from what you wear and how you smell to the way in which you greet potential employers, maintain eye contact during the interview, and close and follow up the interview. Do you communicate confidence and trustworthiness in your demeanor, or are you that interviewee who has a limp handshake and shifty eyes? How do you dress, what do you say, and how do you handle yourself throughout various phases of the interview process? If lunch or dinner is included in the interview, what should you order and how should you mind your table manners? Again, you're onstage and your audience is judging you with a very critical eye.

What's Your Interview I.Q.?

Just how well prepared are you for the job interview? Respond to the following statements by indicating your degree of agreement with each:

SCALE: 5 = strongly agree   2 = disagree
           4 = agree   1 = strongly disagree
           3 = maybe, not certain

1. I know what skills I can offer employers.   5 4 3 2 1

2. I know what skills employers most seek
   in candidates.   5 4 3 2 1

3. I can clearly explain to employers what
   I do well and enjoy doing.   5 4 3 2 1

4. I can explain in 60 seconds why an
   employer should hire me.   5 4 3 2 1

5. I can identify and target employers
   I want to get an interview with.   5 4 3 2 1

6. I can develop a job referral network.   5 4 3 2 1

7. I can prospect for job leads.   5 4 3 2 1

8. I can generate at least one job interview
   for every 10 job search contacts I make.   5 4 3 2 1

9. I can follow up on job interviews.   5 4 3 2 1

10. I can persuade an employer to renegotiate
    my salary after six months on the job.   5 4 3 2 1

11. I know which questions interviewers are
    most likely to ask me.   5 4 3 2 1

12. If asked to reveal my weaknesses, I know how
    to respond – answer honestly, but always
    stress my strengths.   5 4 3 2 1

13. I know how to best dress for the interview.   5 4 3 2 1

14. I know the various types of interviews I may
    encounter and how to appropriately respond
    in each situation.   5 4 3 2 1

15. I can easily approach strangers for job
    information and advice.   5 4 3 2 1

16. I know where to find information on
    organizations that are most likely to be
    interested in my skills.   5 4 3 2 1

17. I know how to go beyond vacancy announce-
    ments to locate job opportunities appropriate
    for my qualifications.   5 4 3 2 1

18. I know how to interview appropriate
    people for job information and advice.   5 4 3 2 1

19. I know many people who can refer me to
    others for informational interviews.   5 4 3 2 1

20. I can uncover jobs on the hidden job market.   5 4 3 2 1

21. I know how to prepare and practice for the
    critical job interview.   5 4 3 2 1

22. I know how to stress my positives.   5 4 3 2 1

23. I know how to research the organization and
    individuals who are likely to interview me.   5 4 3 2 1

24. I have considered how I would respond to
    illegal questions posed by prospective employers.   5 4 3 2 1

25. I can telephone effectively for job leads.   5 4 3 2 1

26. I am prepared to conduct an effective
    telephone interview.   5 4 3 2 1

27. I know when and how to deal with salary
    questions.   5 4 3 2 1

28. I know what to read while waiting in the
    outer office prior to the interview.   5 4 3 2 1

29. I can nonverbally communicate my interest
    and enthusiasm for the job.   5 4 3 2 1

30. I know the best time to arrive at the
    interview site.   5 4 3 2 1

31. I know how to respond using positive form
    and content as well as supports when
    responding to interviewers' questions.   5 4 3 2 1

32. I know how to summarize my strengths
    and value at the closing of the interview.   5 4 3 2 1

33. I know what to include in a thank-you letter.   5 4 3 2 1

34. I know when and how to follow up the
    job interview.   5 4 3 2 1

35. I know what do during the 24- to 48-hour
    period following a job offer.   5 4 3 2 1

36. I can clearly explain to interviewers what
    I like and dislike about particular jobs.   5 4 3 2 1

37. I can explain to interviewers why I made
    my particular educational choices, including
    my major and grade point average.   5 4 3 2 1

38. I can clearly explain to interviewers what
    I want to be doing 5 or 10 years from now.   5 4 3 2 1

39. I have a list of references who can speak in
    a positive manner about me and my work
    abilities.   5 4 3 2 1

40. I can clearly state my job and career
    objectives as both skills and outcomes.   5 4 3 2 1

41. I have set aside 20 hours a week to primarily
    conduct informational interviews.   5 4 3 2 1

42. I know what foods and drinks are best to
    select if the interview includes a luncheon
    or dinner meeting.   5 4 3 2 1

43. I know how to listen effectively.   5 4 3 2 1

44. I can explain why an employer should hire me.   5 4 3 2 1

45. I am prepared to handle the salary question
    at whatever point it comes up.   5 4 3 2 1

46. I know when to use my resume in an informa-
    tional interview.   5 4 3 2 1

47. I can generate three new job leads each day.   5 4 3 2 1

48. I can outline my major achievements in my
    last three jobs and show how they relate to
    the job I am interviewing for.   5 4 3 2 1

49. I know what the interviewer is looking for
    when he or she asks about my weaknesses.   5 4 3 2 1

50. I am prepared to handle both serial and
    stress interviews.   5 4 3 2 1

TOTAL I.Q. [   ]

Once you have completed this exercise, add your responses to compute a total score. This will comprise your composite I.Q. If your score is between 200 and 250, you seem well prepared to successfully handle the interview. If your score is between 150 and 199, you are heading in the right direction, and many of our recommended resources should help you increase your interview competencies. If your score falls below 150, you have a great deal of work to do in preparation for the job interview.

Interview Sins and Knockouts

Unlike many other job search mistakes, interview errors tend to be unforgiving. This is the time when first impressions count the most.

Employers have both positive and negative goals in mind. On the positive side, they want to hire someone who can do the job and add value or benefits to their organization. On the negative side, they are always looking for clues that tell them why they should **not** hire you. After all, you are probably another stranger who makes inflated claims about your competence in the hope of getting a job offer. It's not until you start performing on the job that the employer gets to see the "real you" and discover your patterns of behavior. In the meantime, the employer needs to be on his or her guard looking for evidence that you may be the wrong person for the job. Make a mistake during the job interview and you may be instantly eliminated from further consideration. Therefore, you must be on your very best behavior and avoid the many common mistakes interviewees make.

*Employers also look for clues that tell them why they should **not** hire you.*

The following mistakes are frequently cited by employers who have interviewed hundreds of applicants:

1. **Arrives late to the interview.** First impressions really do count and they are remembered for a long time. Arrive late and you've made one of the worst impressions possible! Indeed, regardless of what you say or do during the interview, you may never recover from this initial mistake. Employers wonder, *"Will you also come to work late?"*

2. **Makes a bad impression in the waiting area.** Treats receptionists and secretaries as inferiors – individuals who may have important input into the hiring process when later asked by the employer *"What was your impression of this candidate?"* Caught reading frivolous materials – *People Magazine* – in the waiting area when company reports and related literature were readily available.

3. **Offers stupid excuses for behavior.** Excuses are usually red flags indicating that a person is unwilling to take responsibility and do the work. Here's a killer excuse for arriving late for a job interview: *"I got lost because your directions weren't very clear."* Goodbye! Here are some other classic excuses heard during job interviews:

   - I forgot.
   - It wasn't my fault.
   - It was a bad company.
   - My boss was a real jerk.
   - The college wasn't very good.
   - I can't remember why I did that.
   - No one there appreciated my work.
   - I didn't have time to visit your website.
   - I'm not a job hopper – I'm getting lots of experience.

4. **Presents a poor appearance and negative image.** Dresses inappropriately for the interview – under-dresses or over-dresses for the position. In some cases the interviewee may just be a country bumpkin – chooses poor quality clothing, selects inappropriate colors, and looks like a clown. He or she may need to learn some basic grooming habits, from haircut and style to makeup and nails, or undergo a major makeover.

5. **Expresses bad, negative, and corrosive attitudes.** Tends to be negative, overbearing, extremely aggressive, cynical, and opinionated to the extreme. Expresses intolerance and strong prejudices toward others. Complains a lot about everything and everybo dy. In Yiddish such ch ronic complainers are

known as *kvetchers*. Indicates a possible caustic personality that will not fit in well with the company. Regardless of how talented this person may be, unless he works in a cell by himself, he'll probably be fired within two months for having a bad attitude that pollutes the office and harms morale.

6. **Engages in inappropriate and unexpected behaviors for an interview situation.** Shows off scars, tattoos, muscles, or pictures of family. Flirts with the interviewer. Possibly an exhibitionist who may also want to date the boss and harass co-workers!

7. **Appears somewhat incoherent and unfocused.** Tends to offer incomplete thoughts, loses focus, and jumps around to unrelated ideas. Hard to keep a focused conversation going. Incoherent thought processes indicate a possible attention deficit disorder (ADD) problem.

8. **Inarticulate.** Speaks poorly, from sound of voice and diction to grammar, vocalized pauses, and jargon. Uses lots of *"you know," "ah," "like," "okay,"* and *"well"* fillers. Expresses a low-class street language – *"cool," "damn," "man," "wow."* Not a good candidate for using the telephone or interacting with clients. Appears verbally illiterate. Writing is probably similar.

9. **Gives short and incomplete answers to questions.** Tends to respond to most questions with *"Yes," "No," "Maybe,"* or *"I'm not sure"* when the interviewer expects more in-depth answers. Appears shallow and indicates a lack of substance, initiative, interest, and enthusiasm.

10. **Lacks a sense of direction.** Appears to have no goals or apparent objectives. Just looking for a job and paycheck rather than pursuing a passion or cause.

11. **Appears ill or has a possible undisclosed medical condition.** Looks pale, glassy-eyed, gaunt, or yellow. Coughs, sneezes, and sounds terrible. Talks about her upcoming operation – within six weeks of starting the job! Prospect employer

suspects this person may have an illness or a drug and alcohol addiction.

12. **Volunteers personal information that normally would be illegal or inappropriate to ask.** Candidate makes interviewer feel uncomfortable by talking about religion, political affiliation, age, family, divorce, sexual orientation, and physical and mental health. Volunteers red flags that knock the candidate out of the competition.

13. **Emits bad or irritating smells.** Reeks of excessive perfume, cologne, or shaving lotion – could kill mosquitos! Can smell smoke or alcohol on breath. Strong body order indicates personal hygiene problems. Has bad breath throughout the interview, which gets cut short for an unexplained reason!

14. **Shows little enthusiasm, drive, or initiative.** Appears to be just looking for a job and a paycheck. Tends to be passive and indifferent. No evidence of being a self-starter who takes initiative and solves problems on his own. Not sure what motivates this person other than close supervision. Indeed, he'll require lots of supervision or we'll have an employee with lots of play-time on his hands, or the company will expand to fill the time allotted. He'll become the "job guy" who always says *"I did my job just like you told me,"* but not much beyond what's assigned. Don't expect much from this person, who will probably be overpaid for what he produces.

15. **Lacks confidence and self-esteem.** Seems unsure of self, nervous, and ill at ease. Lacks decisiveness in making decisions. Communicates uncertainly with such comments as *"I don't know," "Maybe," "I'm not sure," "Hadn't really thought of that," "Interesting question," "I'll have to think about that,"* or redirects with the question *"Well, what do you think?"*

16. **Appears too eager and hungry for the job.** Is overly enthusiastic, engages in extreme flattery, and appears suspiciously nervous. Early in the interview, before learning much about the company or job, makes such comments as *"I really*

like it here," "I need this job," "Is there overtime?," "What are you paying?," "How many vacation days do you give?"

17. **Communicates dishonesty or deception.** Uses canned interview language, evades probing questions, and appears disingenuous. Looks like a tricky character who has things to hide and thus will probably be sneaky and deceptive on the job.

18. **Feels too smooth and superficial.** Dresses nicely, has a firm handshake and good eye contact, answers most questions okay, and appears enthusiastic – just like the books tell job seekers to do. When asked more substantive *"What if"* and behavior-based questions, or requested to give examples of specific accomplishments, the candidate seems to be caught off balance and stumbles with incomplete answers. Can't put one's finger on the problem, but the gut reaction is that this role-playing candidate is very superficial and will probably end up being the "dressed for success" and "coached for the interview" employee from hell!

19. **Appears evasive when asked about possible problems with background.** Gives elusive answers to red flag questions about frequent job changes, termination, and time gaps in work history. Such answers raise questions about the interviewee's honesty, credibility, sense of responsibility, and overall behavior. Indicates a possible negative behavior pattern that needs further investigation. On second thought, don't waste time investigating such candidates, who are more trouble than they are worth.

20. **Speaks negatively of previous employers and co-workers.** When asked why he left previous employers, usually responds by bad-mouthing them. Has little good to say about others who apparently were not as important as this candidate.

21. **Maintains poor eye contact.** At least in North America, eye contact is an indication of trustworthiness and attention.

Individuals who fail to maintain an appropriate amount of eye contact are often judged as untrustworthy – have something to hide. Having too little or too much eye contact during the interview gives off mixed messages about what you are saying. Worst of all, it may make the interviewer feel uncomfortable in your presence.

22. **Offers a limp or overly firm handshake.** Interviewers often get two kinds of handshakes from candidates – the wimps and the bone-crushers. Your initial handshake may say something about your personality. Candidates offering a cold, wet, and limp handshake often come across as corpses! Bone-crushers may appear too aggressive.

23. **Shows little interest in the company.** Indicates he didn't do much research, since he knows little about the company and didn't have time to check out the company's website. Asks this killer question: *"What do you do here?"* Goodbye, again!

24. **Talks about salary and benefits early in the interview.** Rather than try to learn more about the company and position as well as demonstrate her value, the candidate seems preoccupied with salary and benefits by talking about them within the first 15 minutes of the interview. Shows little interest in the job or employer beyond the compensation package. When the interviewee prematurely starts to talk about compensation, red flags go up again – this is a self-centered candidate who is not really interested in doing the job or advancing a career.

25. **Is discourteous, ill-mannered, and disrespectful.** Arrives for the interview a half hour late with no explanation or a phone call indicating a problem en route. Just sits and waits for the interviewer to ask questions. Picks up things on the interviewer's desk. Bites nails and picks nose during the interview. Challenges the interviewer's ideas. Closes the interview without thanking the interviewer for the opportunity to interview for the job. Not even going to charm and etiquette school would help this candidate!

26. **Tells inappropriate jokes and laughs a lot.** Attempts at humor bomb – appears to be a smart ass who likes to laugh at his own jokes. Comes across as an irritating clown who says stupid and silly things. Will need to frequently put this one out to pasture to keep him away from other employees who don't share such humor.

27. **Talks too much.** Can't answer a question without droning on and on with lots of irrelevant talk. Volunteers all kinds of information, including interesting but sensitive personal observations and gossip, the interviewer neither needs nor wants. Doesn't know when to shut up. Would probably waste a lot of valuable work time talking, talking, and talking and thus irritating other employees. Seems to need lots of social strokes through talk which she readily initiates.

28. **Drops names to impress the interviewer.** Thinks the interviewer will be impressed with a verbal Rolodex of who he knows. But interviewers tend to be put off with such candidates who, instead, appear insecure, arrogant, and patronizing – three deadly sins that may shorten your interview from 45 minutes to 15 minutes!

29. **Appears needy and greedy.** Talks a lot about financial needs and compensation. When discussing salary, talks about his personal financial situation, including debts and planned future purchases, rather than what the job is worth and what value he will bring to the job. Seems to expect the employer is interested in supporting his lifestyle, which may be a combination of irresponsible financial behavior, failing to plan (including family planning), living beyond his pay grade, and having bad luck. This line of talk indicates he probably has debilitating financial problems that go far beyond the salary level of this job. Not interested in paying for his needs.

30. **Closes the interview by just leaving.** How you close the interview may determine whether or not you will be invited back to another interview or offered the job. Most interviewees

fail to properly close interviews. A proper close should include these six elements:

1. Indicate you are indeed interested in the job.
2. Summarize what you see as your major strengths and future contributions to the company.
3. Thank the interviewer for his or her time.
4. Ask when they plan to make the final hiring decision.
5. Shake hands and say *"I hope to hear from you soon. Would it be okay to call you next week?"*
6. Leave with a smile on your face and a spring to your step – positive body language as you exit.

Never ever close the interview with this stupid and presumptuous closing prior to being offered the job: *"So when can I start?"* This question will finish off the interview and your candidacy – you're back to being needy and greedy! Also, don't play the pressure game, even if it's true, by stating *"I have another interview this week. When can I expect to hear from you?"* One other critical element to this close: send a nice thank-you letter within 24 hours in which you again express your appreciation for the interview and your interest in the job.

31. **Fails to talk about accomplishments.** Candidate concentrates on explaining work history as primarily consisting of assigned duties and responsibilities. When asked to give examples of her five major accomplishments in her last jobs, doesn't seem to understand the question, gives little evidence of performance, or reverts once again to discussing formal duties and responsibilities. When probed further for accomplishments, can't really say much and shows discomfort about this line of questioning.

32. **Does not ask questions about the job or employer.** When asked *"Do you have any questions?,"* replies *"No"* or *"You've covered everything."* Asking questions is often more important than answering questions. When you ask thoughtful questions, you emphasize your interest in the employer and

job as well as indicate your intelligence – qualities employers look for in candidates.

33. **Appears self-centered rather than employer-centered.** This will become immediately apparent by the direction of the answers and questions coming from the interviewee. If they primarily focus on benefits to the interviewee, the candidate will tend to be self-centered. For example, a candidate who frequently uses "I" when talking about himself and the job may be very self-centered. On the other hand, the candidate who talks about "we" and "you" is usually more employer-oriented. Contrast these paired statements about the job and compensation:

> *"What would I be doing in this position?"*

> *"What do you see us achieving over the next six months?"*

or

> *"What would I be making on this job?"*

> *"What do you normally pay for someone with my qualifications?"*

34. **Demonstrates poor listening skills.** Doesn't listen carefully to questions or seems to have her own agenda that overrides the interviewer's interest. Tends to go off in different directions from the questions being asked. Not a very empathetic listener both verbally and nonverbally. Seems to be more interested in talking about own agenda than focusing on the issues at hand. Apparently wants to take charge of the interview and be the Lone Ranger. The job really does require good listening skills!

35. **Seems not too bright for the job.** Answering simple interview questions is like giving an intelligence test. Has difficulty talking about past accomplishments. Doesn't seem to grasp what the job is all about or the skills required. Seems

confused and lacks focus. Should never have gotten to the job interview but had a terrific looking resume which was probably written by a professional resume writer for $300!

36. **Fails to know his/her worth and negotiate properly when it comes time to talk about compensation.** Job seekers are well advised to only talk about salary and benefits after being offered the job. If you prematurely talk about compensation, you may diminish your value as well as appear self-centered. Be sure to research salary comparables so you know what you are worth in today's job market (start with www.salary.com). Listen carefully throughout the interview and ask questions that would give you a better idea of what the job is actually worth. Emphasize throughout the interview your skills and accomplishments – those things that are most valued by employers who are willing to pay what's necessary for top talent. When you do start negotiating, let the employer state a salary figure first and then negotiate using salary ranges to reach common ground. These and other salary negotiation techniques are outlined in several books on salary negotiations as well as on several websites (see the list of resources at the end of this chapter).

37. **Fails to properly prepare for the interview.** This is the most important mistake of all. It affects all the other mistakes. Indeed, failing to prepare will immediately show when the candidate makes a bad first impression, fails to indicate knowledge about the company and job, gives poor answers to standard interview questions, and does not ask questions. In other words, the candidate makes many of the mistakes outlined above because he or she failed to anticipate what goes into a winning interview. Since you should be communicating your very best self during the interview, failing to prepare for it says something about how you deal with important things in your life and work. In this case, the employer and job were not important enough for you to prepare properly. That's okay. The employer now knows the real serious you.

Books and Websites on Interviewing

Interview preparation is essential for conducting a winning interview. Fortunately, numerous books and websites are available to help job seekers improve their interview skills.

Books on Job Interviewing

101 Dynamite Questions to Ask at Your Job Interview
101 Great Answers to the Toughest Interview Questions
250 Job Interview Questions You'll Most Likely Be Asked
Adams Job Interview Almanac, with CD-ROM)
Don't Blow the Interview
Everything Practice Interview Book
Haldane's Best Answers to Tough Interview Questions
I Can't Believe Thay Asked Me That!
Interview Rehearsal Book
Job Interview Tips for People With Not-So-Hot Backgrounds
Job Interviews for Dummies
KeyWords to Nail Your Job Interview
Nail the Job Interview
Naked at the Interview
The Perfect Interview
Power Interviews
Savvy Interviewing
Sweaty Palms
Tell Your Story, Win the Job
Win the Interview, Win the Job
Winning Job Interviews
Winning the Interview Game

Interview-Related Websites

- Monster.com   interview.monster.com
- InterviewPro   interviewpro.com
- Job-Interview.net   job-interview.net
- Interview Coach   interviewcoach.com
- Quintessential Careers   quintcareers.com/intvres.html

- Riley Guide   rileyguide.com/netintv.html
- WinningTheJob   winningthejob.com

Several additional books and websites focus on salary negotiations – which should occur **after** receiving a job offer, either at the very end of the interview or in a separate interview session. We summarize these related resources at the end of Chapter 13.

The Face-to-Face Encounter

While much of the job search can be conducted in isolation of people, the job interview puts you face-to-face with potential employers. As such, it requires important communication and social skills – both verbal and nonverbal – that determine whether or not you will be offered the job. If you develop an effective networking campaign (see Chapter 6) that connects you to lots of people with whom you conduct informational interviews, you should be well prepared to handle the face-to-face job interview.

11

Fail to Develop an Attractive Pattern of Work Behavior

W HAT IS YOUR MOST important asset in today's job market? It's your pattern of work behavior. Most everyone, except someone first entering the job market, has some type of work experience. The more experience they have, the clearer their pattern of work behavior. It's this pattern that employers are interested in learning about and projecting into their organization. If, for example, you are a very talented writer and have had a consistent pattern of producing award-winning articles during the past 10 years, chances are you will continue doing so in the future.

People Perform, Patterns Predict

Many job seekers go naked into the job market with little self-knowledge about their patterns of performance. Some rack up a spotty work history of being fired, changing jobs frequently, and performing poorly on jobs because of problems relating to negative attitudes, lack of initiative, failure to listen, errors in work, and insubordination. Some wander around the job market, going from job to job, with difficult and less-than-promising backgrounds. They require some form of professional intervention, such as cognitive behavioral therapy, to get their lives back on track or resign themselves to additional employment failures.

As more and more individuals discover each day, their past eventually catches up with them, in one form or another and often in multiple settings. Employers increasingly do background checks, probe references, and require prospective employees to take tests, including psychological inventories. If you have a criminal record, for example, you know it's extremely difficult to expunge that record; it may follow you everywhere you go, including many minor offenses. Indeed, nearly 700,000 individuals transition from state and federal prisons to the work world each year with such career-damaging records. An additional 10 to 11 million individuals circulate in and out of city and county jails and detention centers each year. Many of them return to prison or jail within the first year. Very few employers want to hire individuals with a pattern of criminality.

> *Your past may eventually catch up with you since employers increasingly do background checks, probe references, and require tests.*

The employers' goal is very simple: try to predict as much as possible your behavior and performance in their organization. Not wishing to host social experiments, they don't have time to rehabilitate troubled individuals who believe "this time" they will do better if only given another chance. Most people don't change their patterns of behavior on the basis of wishful thinking or free will. Their patterns follow them wherever they go and then tend to repeat again and again. Therefore, savvy employers know they had better understand behavior patterns of prospective employees **before** they put them on the payroll. If not, they may be in for disappointing and disruptive results from individuals who managed to "ace" the job interview and then trash the job as old patterns arise in the new work setting.

Identify Your Patterns

What exactly do you know about your work patterns? Can you summarize within two minutes what you consistently do well and enjoy doing? Is it an attractive pattern that will appeal to employers?

Individuals who know their patterns of performance are better able to communicate their qualifications to employers because they speak their language. The best way to identify your pattern of performance is to complete the Motivated Abilities and Skills (MAS) exercise in Chapter 7. By generating data on your achievements and then synthesizing them into skill clusters, you will be able to identify your patterns of performance. After you've completed these exercises, try to develop a list of five positive work patterns that best describe you. For example, you might discover your patterns approximate some of these examples:

Takes initiative in quickly solving problems and putting into place permanent systems for resolving future problems.

Adept problem solver who easily transfers knowledge to teammates.

Detail-oriented professional who responds to customer needs in a timely manner.

Skilled in training sales teams that consistently exceed annual sales targets.

Works well under stressful conditions that simultaneously require multi-tasking and trouble-shooting.

My Major Patterns of Performance

1. _____

   _____

2. _____

   _____

3. _____

   _____

4. _____

   _____

5. _____

_____

Based on an analysis of your accomplishments in Chapter 7, you should be able to give several examples that document each of your patterns. These will be **stories** of what you did, when, with whom, and with what consequences (outcomes or results). These examples should make up a powerful arsenal of performance stories that go far beyond just the anecdotal. They relate to this larger picture of performance. As such, they give substance to your patterns.

Changing Not-So-Hot Patterns

As we noted in Chapter 3, individuals can and do change their attitudes and behaviors. If you feel locked into a not-so-hot pattern of work behavior, you may want to review Chapter 3 on self-transformation through attitude adjustments. You can change your life, but you must first deal with a set of attitudes that may be preventing you from making such changes as well as be motivated to make the necessary changes. Review the many resources on self-transformation on page 49 to see if they can assist in changing your attitudes and behaviors. If not, take another important step to change your life – get professional assistance, which we address in Chapter 17.

Useful Resources

For more information on how to identify your patterns of achievement or performance and tell your stories, see the following books:

Haldane's Best Resumes of Professionals
High Impact Resumes and Letters
Tell Your Story, Win the Job
The Truth About You

People Management, Inc. (www.peoplemanagement.org) also uses a technique called SIMA (System for Identifying Motivated Abilities) for identifying such patterns.

12

Appear Honest But Stupid or Dishonest But Smart

W HAT'S WORSE? ENCOUNTERING someone who is honest but stupid or dishonest but smart. At least for employers, it may not make much difference since the outcomes may be similar – a bad hire with new troubles coming for the workplace. It's not uncommon for employers to meet such candidates who lack good judgment and ethics.

Take the Ethics Quiz

Let's take an ethics quiz on the job search. Respond to the following statements by indicating your degree of agreement with each:

SCALE: 1 = strongly agree   4 = disagree
        2 = agree   5 = strongly disagree
        3 = maybe, not certain

1. Honesty is always the best policy
   when conducting a job search.   1   2   3   4   5

2. Honest people finish last in today's
   competitive job market.   1   2   3   4   5

3. Employers prefer hiring frank and
   honest people who always tell the
   truth, including the whole truth.   1   2   3   4   5

4. Employers are no more honest about
   themselves than candidates. Everyone
   exaggerates on their resume.   1   2   3   4   5

5. I should be up front and tell employers
   early on what I really want – more
   money and better health benefits.   1   2   3   4   5

6. I'll give the employer what he wants –
   a story of someone (me) who he thinks
   can walk on water.   1   2   3   4   5

7. If true, I should indicate on my resume
   or in my cover letter that I was fired
   from my last job.   1   2   3   4   5

8. It's none of the employer's business that
   I was fired. If asked, I'll tell her that I left
   because of a dishonest boss who was likely
   to go to jail!   1   2   3   4   5

9. When asked why I didn't complete school
   I should tell the truth about my problems
   with drugs and alcohol.   1   2   3   4   5

10. When asked why I didn't complete
    school, I'll make up a story about my
    dying mother or a career opportunity
    I couldn't pass up.   1   2   3   4   5

11. I should let the employer know that I'm
    a single mother trying to support three
    small children.   1   2   3   4   5

12. I'll tell the employer I have a great
    family life.   1   2   3   4   5

13. When asked to explain why I have a
    two-year employment gap, I should
    come clean and tell the employer about
    my incarceration for drug dealing. But
    I'm clean now.   1   2   3   4   5

14. When asked to explain why I have a
     two-year employment gap, I'll tell
     the employer I needed to take some
     time off to reassess my career goals.   1   2   3   4   5

15. If true, I should tell the employer that
     I have a bipolar disorder but that I have
     this illness under control with drugs.   1   2   3   4   5

16. If an employer asks any mental health
     questions, I'll try to remain calm and
     remind him that he's asking a totally
     inappropriate question.   1   2   3   4   5

17. I should tell the interviewer that I'm
     pregnant and that I'll need six weeks of
     maternity leave in another six months.   1   2   3   4   5

18. I'll wait until I'm on the job a few weeks
     before telling the employer I need six weeks
     maternity leave starting in September.   1   2   3   4   5

If you agree or strongly agreed with the odd-numbered statements, you
have a propensity to be honest but stupid in the job search. On the other
hand, if you agreed or strongly agreed with the even-numbered statements, you verge on being dishonest but smart. If you're somewhere in
the middle on all of the statements, you may not be making this type of
mistake. Let's elaborate on what we mean by honest but stupid and
dishonest but smart job seekers.

Stupid But Honest

There's no rule that says you must confess your sins and volunteer
negative information about yourself in the job search. That would be
stupid since it might knock you out of consideration for no good reason
other than your own self-destruction. Take, for example, these two
contrasting statements from two candidates who left their last jobs for the
same reason. They tell the truth two different ways:

I didn't get along with my boss.

I thought it was time to move on to more challenging opportunities.

Both statements are 100 percent honest, but the first one is naive and stupid. It labels the person as someone who may have difficulty handling authority and who personalizes workplace issues. The second statement is honest and professional. It emphasizes that the candidate may have professional goals and a larger vision of where she wants to go career-wise. If given a choice, employers would shy away from hiring the first candidate. The second candidate has what employers desire – honesty, professionalism, and tact.

While employers definitely want honest and sincere employees, they are not particularly attracted to brutally frank employees who mistake their frankness for honesty. Indeed, some of the most honest people say the stupidest things about themselves to others. They confess their sins, volunteer negative information about themselves, and reveal personal details that make others uncomfortable. Indeed, they may become living soap operas with revealing tales of their many struggles to survive and prosper against so many odds. Such frankness

> *There's no rule that says you must confess your sins and volunteer negative information about yourself in the job search.*

is inappropriate in a job search. It sets you up for failure by accurately labeling you for what you really are – honest but stupid. Employers cannot afford to hire such people.

Employers want you to be truthful about your education, training, skills, and accomplishments as they relate to the job and workplace. They are not really interested in getting involved in the trials and tribulations of your personal life, however interesting it may be to you. Those are inappropriate and uncomfortable subjects for employers. Don't bore them with the details of your marriage, family, health, religion, politics, and travel.

Dishonest But Smart

Employers seem to increasingly encounter dishonest but smart candidates who deliberately lie on their resumes and in interviews. Indeed, recent studies on verifying claims on resumes have indicated that over 50 percent of job seekers lie on their resumes, from educational credentials to job titles, employers, and employment dates. Many candidates feel compelled to make up dishonest or deceptive stories in order to get the interview and job offer.

Too many employers have been burnt by such candidates to rely only on the resume and interviews for making hiring decisions. Except for very small companies that often neglect to do their screening homework, more and more employers are hiring smarter as they increasingly use outside groups to verify credentials, ask more probing questions of references, and subject candidates to testing, including psychological profiles and polygraphs. The days of dishonest but smart job seekers may be numbered, especially with employers who do their homework in screening candidates.

Dishonest but smart job seekers should be forewarned that there is a high probability of catching their deception in today's security-conscious job market. Many employers simply expect to be lied to by candidates. They will check you out. If not, they will probably discover your pattern of deception once you're on the job. Indeed, dishonest but smart job seekers have a habit of making revealing mistakes on the job.

13

Project an Image of Need or Greed

O NE OF THE BIGGEST MISTAKES job seekers make is to appear needy or greedy, especially during the job interview. Remember, employers want to know what it is you will do for them – your performance in exchange for their compensation. On the other hand, you should be trying to acquire as much information on the employer and the job to decide whether or not you want the position. It's only after you and the employer have had a chance to assess each other should you begin talking about compensation. At that point, both parties should have a good idea what both you and the position are worth. At least this is the ideal way to approach the subject.

Premature Money Talk

Overly concerned about money, many job seekers forget what they should be trying to do and thus prematurely raise the money issue in the job search. In fact, some start out early on by stating their salary requirements on their resume or in the cover letter. Others get a screening call from an employer and ask *"What are you paying?"* And still others talk about money during the first five minutes of the job interview!

Prematurely talking about money has two unfortunate consequences for job seekers:

1. **You appear needy or greedy in the eyes of many employers, who need to know more about you before talking about real money.** They may respond by saying *"It depends on your qualifications,"* since they are not finished assessing your qualifications. They know what the position has been worth in the past, but they're not yet sure what **you** are worth. They may be less certain what other comparable employers are paying for similar positions. On the other hand, they may throw out a salary figure, which will most likely be their low end of a range, to see how you react. Your money question may leave a bad impression on the employer, who thinks you are primarily interested in money rather than the job.

2. **You may show your hand early in the game and thus lose the advantage when it comes time to negotiate compensation, which should be right after you receive a job offer.** By asking the salary question, you set yourself up for failure. If, for example, the employer responds by saying *"We've budgeted this position at $40,000,"* how will you respond so early in the job interview? You know hardly anything about the position, the employer, and your level of responsibilities. How can you intelligently respond to that question except from a perspective of need or greed: *"I really need to be making $50,000 because of my new car payments"*? That will really impress the employer! But what if you later learn the job was really worth $60,000 but you continued to interview for the job knowing full well that the employer was offering $40,000. Now what will you do since you already popped the money question before you had a chance to value the position? The employer thinks you're on board for a $40,000 position.

Whatever you do, avoid the impression of being a needy or greedy job seeker who is primarily interested in money. You'll eventually get to the money question, but your timing must be right for you to be in a position of strength when it comes time to negotiate a compensation package.

Needy/Greedy Job Seekers

When it comes time to talk about compensation, what rationale will you present for the salary you are expecting? Needy and greedy job seekers tend to personalize the salary question. Rather that talk about the value of their skills and accomplishments in reference to the value of the position, they wander off into personal territory. Like our honest but stupid job seeker in Chapter 12, they talk about their personal needs. Here's what many job seekers give as reasons to justify a particular salary figure they wish to receive:

1. _I need to make at least 15 percent more than on my last job._

2. _I'm buying a new car, so I'll need to make at least $200 more a month to meet my new car payments._

3. _My expenses will go up with the new baby in December._

4. _We're buying a new home and it will be tough with this salary._

5. _My son is going to college in the fall. You wouldn't believe the cost of tuition. We'll have difficulty making ends meet!_

These are all personal need and greed statements rationalizing compensation requests. While they may be true, they should never be shared with an employer, who believes you should be compensated for your performance rather than according to your financial needs. This is the type of unprofessional rationale that can easily knock you out of consideration.

Negotiate Right

You will be in a much stronger negotiation position if you focus on the job and keep the money question to the very end. Here's what you need to do if you want to be in a strong negotiation position to get the best possible compensation package:

1. **Avoid talking about salary until after you receive a job offer.** If the employer brings up the question early in the job interview (*"What are your salary requirements?"*), put him off by saying *"I would rather talk about that later after we've had a chance to discuss the position and how I would fit into the organization."*

2. **Conduct compensation research to learn about salary and benefit comparables for similar positions.** Several salary websites on page 153, such as salary.com, should prove useful for gathering such data, along with salary data gathered by your state employment office, professional associations, and other groups. Be sure to thoroughly investigate benefits.

3. **Let the employer state the first figure.** If the employer asks *"What are your salary requirements?,"* respond by turning the question around: *"What do you normally pay for someone with my qualifications?"* Remember the old poker rule: *"He who shows his hand first loses the advantage."*

4. **Talk about a salary range rather than a specific figure.** If you really want the job, it's best to negotiate within ranges which enable you to reach common ground. For example, if the employer says *"$45,000,"* you might respond by stating a range that puts this figure at the bottom and thereby creates common ground from which to negotiate: *"I was thinking in the range of $45,000 to $55,000."* Once you establish a range, you have room to negotiate toward the upper end of the range.

5. **Reach agreement, summarize, and close.** If, for example, you agree on $55,000, end the negotiation session by summarizing what you understand will be your duties and responsibilities and ask that this all be put into a letter of intent. Follow up with a nice thank-you letter expressing your enthusiasm, gratitude, and interest in joining the company.

   Whatever you do, negotiate your salary from a professional position of strength by focusing on the value of both you and the position. Avoid any talk that hints of need or greed.

Resources on Salary Negotiations

Several books and websites prepare job seekers for negotiating salaries. You need to concentrate on conducting research on salary comparables and negotiation strategies that put you in a strong position for getting what you believe you and the position are really worth.

Books on Salary Negotiations

101 Salary Secrets
Are You Paid What You're Worth?
Dynamite Salary Negotiations
Get More Money On Your Next Job
Get Paid What You're Worth
Get a Raise in 7 Days
Negotiating Your Salary
Negotiating Your Job Offer
Perfect Phrases for Negotiating Salary and Job Offers
Salary Negotiation Tips for Professionals
Secrets of Power Salary Negotiating

Salary-Related Websites

- Salary.com   salary.com
- JobStar.org   jobstar.org
- Wageweb   www.wageweb.com
- Abbott-Langer   abbott-langer.com
- Robert Half International   www.rhii.com
- Monster.com   salary.monster.com
- SalarySource.com   salarysource.com
- Quintessential Careers   quintcareers.com/salary_
                                 negotiation.html
- Riley Guide   rileyguide.com/netintv.html
- WinningTheJob   winningthejob.com
- SalaryExpert   salaryexpert.com

14

Conduct an Outdated Job Search or Over-Rely on Technology

NUMEROUS CHANGES HAVE taken place in the job market and with job search strategies during the past 20 years. Many of the changes are technological in nature, especially with the increasing role of the Internet in recruiting candidates and conducting a job search. But the changes are much more than technological. The most important changes are conceptual and involve the use of smart job search strategies, many of which we have discussed in previous chapters of this book.

Outdated Versus Updated Job Search

A traditional outdated job search is characterized by many of the myths outlined in Chapter 9 on conducting a resume-based job search. Such a job search is basically a passive writing and mailing activity involving the submission of resumes and letters in response to classified ads. If such job seekers incorporate the Internet into their job search, they do so passively by primarily identifying job postings, submitting resumes to online databases, and emailing letters. Individuals using this approach spend a lot of time **waiting** for responses from employers. If you conduct such an outdated job search in today's job market, you're in trouble. Indeed, many people using this approach are our frustrated job seekers who complain *"No one will hire me!"* And why would they if you're using such a waiting approach that didn't even work well 20 years ago?

An updated job search is one that is very proactive. It's centered around the whole seven-step job search process we outlined in Chapter 4. The foundation of a proactive job search is self-assessment and goal setting. Once you know what you do well and enjoy doing and formulate a job objective, you should be well prepared to take purposeful action in the form of research, networking, resume writing and distribution, interviewing, and negotiating salary. This type of job search also incorporates the smart use of the Internet for conducting research, networking for information and advice, identifying vacancies, and submitting resumes online. It's a totally integrated A to Z job search that is designed to clearly communicate your qualifications to targeted employers. It's a job search that

> *Individuals using a traditional outdated job search approach spend lots of time waiting for responses from employers.*

works well in today's rapidly changing job market where employers are looking for top talent and where job seekers are looking for satisfying jobs and careers. Such a proactive job search makes the right connections between candidates and employers.

The chart on page 156 compares the characteristics of a traditional outdated job search with the characteristics of an updated job search.

Over-Reliance on Technology

Just because you use computer software or the Internet to conduct your job search is no reason to conclude you are conducting an updated, smart, and effective job search. Smart job seekers can quickly out-perform you with a pen and typewriter! Any technology is only as good as the person who uses it in the right manner. Indeed, many job seekers use computer software and the Internet to conduct a traditional outdated job search. Rather than focus on classified ads in the newspaper, they shift their focus to classified ads on the Internet – the medium may change but classified ads are classified ads, the bread and butter of the advertised job market

Characteristics of Outdated Versus Updated Job Search

Outdated Job Search	Updated Job Search
■ Passive job search.	■ Proactive job search.
■ Self-centered approach.	■ Employer-centered approach.
■ Primarily focuses on writing and distributing resumes and letters in response to job listings.	■ Focuses on entire job search process, with self-assessment and goal-setting playing important foundation roles.
■ Develops traditional chronological resume stressing employment dates and focusing on duties and responsibilities.	■ Develops performance-oriented resume stressing accomplishments and including an objective and summary of qualifications.
■ Brief cover letter politely repeats the contents of resume.	■ Cover letter expresses personality and includes a follow-up statement.
■ Major job search activities involve responding to classified ads with a resume and letter.	■ Research, networking, and follow-up play critical roles throughout the job search process.
■ Prepares answers to anticipated interview questions.	■ Prepares to both answer and ask questions at the interview.
■ Waits to hear from employers.	■ Uses effective follow-up techniques.
■ Primarily a paper, writing, and mailing exercise.	■ Focuses on email, telephone, and face-to-face communications.
■ Job search tends to be spontaneous and serendipitous.	■ Planning and preparation play key roles throughout the job search.
■ Myth-based job search.	■ Reality-based job search.
■ Little use of the Internet beyond checking online job postings and and posting resumes online.	■ Fully integrates the Internet into the job search, with special emphasis on conducting research and networking.

where owners of newspapers and websites make their money from employers who purchase listings or postings. Or they use computer software to produce a traditional chronological resume or post a similar type of ineffective resume to an online database. While they may feel they are conducting an updated job search because of all the technological trappings, in fact they are doing just the opposite: the technology allows them to enlarge the scope of their traditional and ineffective job search!

Using the Internet Properly

If you really want to conduct an updated job search that wisely incorporates the Internet, you should do the following:

1. **Don't spend more than 20 percent of your job search time on the Internet.** If you devote more time than that, you are probably wasting your time engaged in wishful thinking. In fact, no more than 15 percent of job seekers actually get jo bs thro ugh their Internet-based jo b s earch activities.

2. **Focus most of your Internet time on conducting research and networking for information, advice, and referrals.** The real strength of the Internet lies in its tremendous search and retrieval capabilities for conducting research and for sending messages, including resumes and letters, via email.

3. **Survey the major employment websites**. Over 25,000 websites in the United States deal with employment. Yes, there's a jungle out there in cyberspace as many job seekers face a daunting task of deciding which sites to visit and possibly use. A good starting point for making such decisions is the AIRS gateway site to job boards:

   airsdirectory.com/jobboards

   This site includes over 6,500 job boards which are classified by industry, function, occupations and other useful categories. In the end, however, you'll probably want to concentrate on several of the most popular employment websites and then select a few sites from the AIRS directory that specialize in your occupational field:

▪ America's Job Bank	www.ajb.org
▪ Monster.com	monster.com
▪ JobCentral	jobcentral.com
▪ CareerBuilder	careerbuilder.com
▪ NationJob	nationjob.com
▪ FlipDog	www.flipdog.com
▪ Hot Jobs	hotjobs.yahoo.com
▪ Employment911.com	employment911.com
▪ CareerJournal	careerjournal.com
▪ CareerFlex	careerflex.com
▪ EmploymentSpot	employmentspot.com
▪ JobFactory	jobfactory.com
▪ WorkTree.com	worktree.com
▪ Job Sniper	jobsniper.com
▪ PlanetRecruit	planetrecruit.com
▪ Vault.com	vault.com
▪ WetFeet.com	wetfeet.com
▪ EmploymentGuide	employmentguide.com
▪ Jobs.com	jobs.com
▪ BestJobsUSA	bestjobsusa.com
▪ Career Shop	careershop.com
▪ MonsterTRAK	monstertrak.com
▪ Career.com	career.com
▪ JobBank USA	jobbankusa.com
▪ Net-Temps	net-temps.com
▪ Job Search USA	jobsearchusa.org
▪ CareerTV	careertv.net
▪ MRINetwork.com	mrinetwork.com
▪ NowHiring.com	nowhiring.com
▪ American Preferred Jobs	preferredjobs.com
▪ ProHire	prohire.com
▪ CareerExchange	careerexchange.com
▪ Career Magazine	careermag.com
▪ Employers Online	employersonline.com

▪ JobCenterUSA	jobcenterusa.com
▪ Arbita	recruitusa.com
▪ Recruiters Online Network	recruitersonline.com
▪ kForce.com	kforce.com
▪ Dice.com	dice.com
▪ Washington Post	www.washingtonjobs. com/wl.jobs/
▪ TrueCareers	truecareers.com
▪ 6FigureJobs	sixfigurejobs.com
▪ ExecuNet	execunet.com
▪ BrassRing	brassring.com
▪ CampusCareerCenter	campuscareercenter.com
▪ College Central Network	collegecentral.com
▪ Jobcircle	jobcircle.com
▪ Prohire	prohire.com
▪ LatPro	latpro.com
▪ Saludos.com	saludos.com

4. **Visit the large employment websites, but don't put much hope in their ability to locate a job or employer for you.** Large employment websites such as <u>Monster.com</u>, <u>HotJobs.yahoo.com</u>, and <u>CareerBuilder.com</u> offer a wealth of information and services to both employers and job seekers. However, these sites are primarily run for the benefit of the paying customers – employers. Job seekers can post their resumes o nline, browse job postings, and apply for jobs through these sites, but few ever get jobs through these sites. The most valuable aspects of these sites for job seekers are the peripheral services which are designed to keep you coming back again and again (in this online business, you're known as "traffic" when sites set their advertising rates for employers):

- ▪ Job Search Tips
- ▪ Featured Articles
- ▪ Career Experts or Advisors
- ▪ Career Tool Kit
- ▪ Career Assessment Tests
- ▪ Community Forums
- ▪ Discussion or Chat Groups

- Message Boards
- Job Alert ("Push") Emails
- Company Research Centers
- Networking Forums
- Salary Calculators or Wizards
- Resume Management Center
- Resume and Cover Letter Advice
- Multimedia Resume Software
- Job Interview Practice
- Relocation Information
- Reference Check Checkers
- Employment or Career News
- Free Email For Privacy
- Success Stories
- Career Newsletter
- Career Events
- Online Job Fairs
- Affiliate Sites
- Career Resources
- Featured Employers
- Polls and Surveys
- Contests
- Online Education and Training
- International Employment
- Talent Auction Centers
- Company Ads (buttons and banners)
- Sponsored Links
- Special Channels for Students, Executives, Freelancers, Military, and other groups

Huge mega employment sites such as <u>Monster.com</u> include over 80 percent of these add-on services. That site alone is well worth visiting again and again for tips and advice. Most sites, however, only include job postings and resume databases and maybe a newsletter designed to capture email addresses of job seekers who must register to receive the newsletter. Again, don't expect too much from these sites in terms of connecting with employers who will invite you to interviews.

5. **Focus on smaller specialty websites relevant to your occupation and industry.** Many users of Internet employment websites focus most of their attention on a few huge employment sites, such as Monster.com and HotJobs.yahoo.com. However, they would be better off using employment websites that specialize in their industry. For example, if you are an IT professional, your chances of connecting with an employer are much greater on dice.com, itcareers.com, and itmoonlighter.com than on the top 10 mega employment sites. Employers interested in hiring IT professionals are more likely to use these specialty sites than the more general mega employment sites.

6. **Move on to job search activities that have a high potential to pay off with invitations to job interviews.** The Internet and employment websites give the deceptive appearance of conducting an up-to-date job search. Used wisely, you should integrate your online research and networking activities with your offline job search activities. As outlined in Chapter 6, networking may prove to be the single most important activity for conducting an effective job search. If you integrate your online research and networking activities with your offline networking activities, you will have a very powerful combination of resources for landing a job you want.

Resources for Using the Internet

Using the Internet in your job search is relatively easy once you have some basic guidance on where to go and what to do. The following books provide details on using the Internet for finding a job. Several of these resources go through the whole process of using the Internet for conducting employment research, posting resumes, and communicating by email. Others primarily annotate the best sites on the Internet:

100 Top Internet Job Sites
Adams Internet Job Search Almanac
America's Top Internet Job Sites
Career Exploration on the Internet
Cyberspace Job Search Kit

The Directory of Websites for International Jobs
The Everything Online Job Search Book
The Guide to Internet Job Searching
Haldane's Best Employment Websites for Professionals
Job-Hunting on the Internet
Job Searching Online for Dummies, With CD-ROM
Weddle's Directory of Employment-Related Internet Sites

Also, be sure to examine these Internet resources, which we earlier discussed in Chapter 9, on writing electronic and Internet resumes:

Best Career and Education Websites
Cyberspace Resume Kit
Electronic Resumes and Online Networking
e-Resumes
Internet Resumes
Job Seeker's Online Goldmine
Resumes in Cyberspace

15

Unwilling to Take Risks and Handle Rejections

HETHER YOU LIKE IT or not, finding a job is about marketing and selling yourself to others, most of whom are strangers. If you are reluctant to approach strangers and talk about yourself in a positive manner – toot your horn – your job search will suffer accordingly. The most important asset in conducting an effective job search is **you**. You must become a successful entrepreneur.

Losing Your Self-Esteem

What are the characteristics of successful entrepreneurs? Above all, they are willing to take risks. And the major risk relates to their ego – the risk of rejection and failure. Eventually being successful, they pick themselves up after each rejection and continue on selling with focus, energy, and drive. Based on their selling experience, they know success awaits them after a few more rejections!

The job search is a highly ego-involved activity requiring similar risk-taking behavior. If, for example, you lost your job, what's the worst thing that could have happened to you? The loss of a paycheck? No office to go to in the morning? Colleagues whom you enjoyed working with? No.

The worst thing that can happen to you is to lose your self-esteem. It's this loss of self-esteem that can endanger your whole job search and kill your entrepreneurial spirit. You feel terrible about yourself. You may think you're a loser whom no one wants to hire. Like other job seekers, you may occasionally go through bouts of depression where you feel worthless and thus have difficulty facing the day and moving your job search ahead with focus and enthusiasm. You have difficulty getting motivated to go out and experience more rejections. So maybe you decide to shortcut the process and retreat behind your computer to conduct an "online job search" or start a resume and letter mailing campaign so you don't have to face people, which you really need to do when you network for information, advice, and referrals. Such passive activities give you a false sense of making progress with your job search.

> *The worst thing that can happen to you is to lose your self-esteem.*

Handling Rejections

Most people are not natural salespeople who can start out the day, be rejected 10 times, and then end the day in an upbeat manner. Most job seekers can absorb about four rejections and then they quit or retreat to less risky types of job search activities, like writing letters and surfing the Internet for jobs. A typical successful job search is all about collecting more rejections than acceptances. In other words, you must persevere against the odds.

What, for example, do you believe your odds are of getting an interview from sending out 100 resumes and letters? 50 percent? 30 percent? 10 percent? 5 percent? Try maybe 1 percent. What about putting your resume into an online database? 1 percent? .001?

If you go into the job search with high expectations that employers are going to come knocking on your door as soon as they learn about your availability, you're living in a field of dreams. The truth is closer to this reality faced by salespeople each day who are committed to meeting with 20 prospects:

1. No	11. Maybe
2. No	12. No
3. No	13. No
4. No	14. No
5. No	15. Yes
6. No	16. No
7. No	17. Maybe
8. No	18. No
9. Maybe	19. No
10. No	20. Yes

Had they quit after the fourth rejection, they would have never gotten to the fifteenth and twentieth prospect that turned into an acceptance. And this is precisely what many job seekers do. They prematurely quit prospecting after their fourth rejection and complain *"There are no jobs out there for me."* Of course not if that's all the effort they make in advancing their job search!

One of the hardest parts of any job search is learning to accept rejections as part of the process rather than taking them personally. You must learn to keep going because the more rejections you collect, the higher the probability you will get acceptances. But acceptances don't come before rejections. Indeed, you should get up in the morning and motivate yourself with this measurable goal:

Today I'm going to go out and collect 20 rejections!

You'll need to stay positive knowing full well that one or two acceptances probably lie somewhere among those 20 rejections. If you can do this, you'll quickly put yourself on the road to job search success. But if you falter after just a few rejections because your ego can't take it, you will have missed out on some great opportunities that lie just a few more *"no's"* ahead!

Minimizing Rejections Through Networking

If you have difficulty approaching and selling yourself to strangers, you will benefit enormously from the networking strategies we outlined in Chapter 6. By conducting informational interviews, you lessen the likelihood of being rejected. You'll be making few cold calls since most of your network contacts come from referrals. Most people will be responsive and assist you with information, advice, and referrals to others, who, in turn, become building blocks in your expanding network. When you use proper networking strategies, your acceptance rates increase significantly and your self-esteem improves accordingly. You'll feel energized and focused to continue your job search in the direction of even more acceptances.

Resources for Handling Rejections

Pick up almost any book or audiocassette on selling and you will learn how to deal with rejections. It's often the centerpiece for selling success. These books and audiocassettes help keep salespeople self-motivated throughout a process that can be very ego-deflating and depressing if rejections become personalized as signs of failure. Once you deal with these two related issues of risk taking and rejection, you'll discover your self-esteem will increase accordingly. Some of the best resources for dealing with this issue are the same resources we identified in Chapter 3 on changing your attitudes through self-transformation.

16

Fail to Implement and Follow Through

T ALK IS CHEAP AND SO ARE books on finding a job. Over the years we have observed an unfortunate pattern of failure. Many job seekers get good advice from career professionals on how to conduct an effective job search, but they simply don't implement or follow through. They say, for example, they will spend 20 hours a week on their job search, but in fact they spend three hours and those three hours are not well used on the most productive job search activities. In the end, failure to implement and follow through may be your number one problem in making this book work for you.

Find Time to Implement

We're going to repeat here what we've said for more than 20 years about success. **Implementation** may be your missing link to achieving success. You've got to find time to implement. And you must implement according to a plan. So here's how to do it. Let's start with better using your time.

Once you've decided to look for a job, you need to find the **time** to properly implement your job search. This requires setting aside specific blocks of time for identifying your motivated abilities and skills, developing your resume, writing letters, making telephone calls, and conducting the necessary research and networking required for success. This whole process takes time. If you are a busy person, like most people, you simply must make the time. Get better organized, give some things up, or cut back on all your activities. If, for example, you can set aside one hour each day to devote to your job search, you will spend seven hours a week or 28 hours a month on your search. However, you should and can find more time than this for these activities.

Time and again we find successful job hunters are the ones who routinize specific job search activities. They make contact after contact, conduct numerous informational interviews, submit many applications and resumes, and keep repeating these activities in spite of encountering rejections. They learn that success is just a few more *"no's"* and informational interviews away. They face each day with a positive attitude fit for someone desiring to change their life – I must collect my ten *"no's"* today because each *"no"* brings me closer to another *"yes"*!

Commit Yourself in Writing

You may find it useful to commit yourself in writing to achieving job search success. This is a very useful way to get both motivated and directed for action. Start by completing the job search contract on page 169 and keep it near you – in your briefcase or on your desk.

In addition, you should complete weekly performance reports. These reports identify what you actually accomplished rather than what your good intentions tell you to do. Make copies of the performance and planning report form on page 170 and use one each week to track your actual progress and to plan your activities for the next week.

If you fail to meet these written commitments, issue yourself a revised and updated contract. But if you do this three or more times, we strongly suggest you stop kidding yourself about your motivation and commitment to find a job. Start over again, but this time consult a professional career counselor who can assist you with your job search. A professional may not be cheap, but if paying for help gets you on the right track and results in the job you want, it's money well spent. Do not be *"penny wise but pound foolish"* with your future. If you must seek professional advice, be sure you are an informed consumer according to our advice on "shopping for a professional" in Chapter 17.

Job Search Contract

1. I'm committed to changing my life by changing my job. Today's date is _____.

2. I will manage my time so that I can successfully complete my job search and find a high quality job. I will begin changing my time management behavior on _____.

3. I will begin my job search on _____.

4. I will involve _____ with my job search.
   (individual/group)

5. I will spend at least one week conducting library research on different jobs, employers, and organizations. I will begin this research during the week of _____.

6. I will complete my skills identification step by _____.

7. I will complete my objective statement by _____.

8. I will complete my resume by _____.

9. Each week I will:

   ■ make _____ new job contacts.

   ■ conduct _____ informational interviews.

   ■ follow up on _____ referrals.

10. My first job interview will take place during the week of _____.

11. I will begin my new job by _____.

12. I will make a habit of learning one new skill each year.

Signature: _____

Date: _____

Weekly Job Performance and Planning Report

1. The week of: _____ .

2. This week I:

   - wrote ____ job search letters.
   - sent ____ resumes and ____ letters to potential employers.
   - completed ____ applications.
   - made ____ job search telephone calls.
   - completed ____ hours of job research.
   - set up ____ appointments for informational interviews.
   - conducted ____ informational interviews.
   - received ____ invitations to a job interview.
   - followed up on ____ contacts and ____ referrals.

3. Next week I will:

   - write ____ job search letters.
   - send ____ resumes and ____ letters to potential employers.
   - complete ____ applications.
   - make ____ job search telephone calls.
   - complete ____ hours of job research.
   - set up ____ appointments for informational interviews.
   - conduct ____ informational interviews.
   - follow up on ____ contacts and ____ referrals.

4. Summary of progress this week in reference to my Job Search Contract commitments:

   _____

   _____

   _____

   _____

   _____

   _____

17

Avoid Professional Advice and Seeking Help

OST PEOPLE CAN USE professional assistance when making critical decisions that affect their future. Finding a job involves such decisions. Our experience is that some job seekers, who are basically self-starters, can conduct their job search on their own without much assistance from others. They can complete the self-directed exercises on identifying their skills, specify an objective, write a winning resume, conduct research, network, and prepare for the interview and salary negotiations on their own. They go on to find a perfect job based on the advice of a job search book.

When You Need Assistance

Few people are self-starters who can read a book and implement it successfully. Some need assistance with each step in the job search process whereas others need assistance with only certain critical steps in the process. For example, you may discover the self-directed self-assessment exercises do not yield enough useful information for specifying your skills and writing strong achievement statements. You may decide you need some sort of career testing, such as the *Myers-Briggs Type Indicator®* and

Strong Interest Inventory® (see Chapters 2 and 8). To do so requires the services of a certified career professional. At the same time, you may struggle with writing your resume according to the advice and examples of several excellent resume writing books. In the end, you decide it's time to spend $300 on the services of a professional resume writer. Our point is that your job search and career are too important to be left to your own devices. You may be *"penny wise but pound foolish"* not to seek professional assistance. Indeed, there is a time and a place to seek professional help.

Alternative Career Services

You'll find at least 12 alternative career planning and employment services. A few are free, but most charge fees. Each has certain advantages and disadvantages. Approach them with caution. Never sign a contract before you read the fine print, get a second opinion, and talk to former clients about the **results** they achieved through the service. With these words of caution, let's take a look at the variety of services available.

1. Public employment services

Public employment services usually consist of a state agency which provides employment assistance as well as dispenses unemployment compensation benefits. Employment assistance largely consists of job listings and counseling services. Most employers still do not list with this service, especially for positions paying more than $40,000 a year. Many of these offices are literally "reinventing" themselves for today's new job market with One-Stop Career Centers (www.career onestop.org), computerized job banks, and other innovative approaches. Many offer useful job services, including self-assessment and job search workshops as well as access to Internet job listings. Most are linked to America's Job Bank (www.ajb.org), an electronic job board which includes job listings throughout the U.S. and abroad, as well as the U.S. Department of Labor's two websites – America's Career InfoNet (www.acinet.org) and America's Learning Exchange (www.servicelocator.org). Veterans will find many of the jobs listed through these offices give veterans preference in hiring. Go see for yourself if your state employment office offers useful services for you.

2. Private employment agencies

Private employment agencies work for money, either from applicants or employers. Approximately 8,000 such agencies operate nation-wide. Many are highly specialized in technical, scientific, and financial fields. The majority serve the interests of employers. While employers normally pay the placement fee, many agencies charge applicants 10 to 15 percent of their first year salary. These firms have one major advantage: job leads which you may have difficulty uncovering elsewhere. The major disadvantages are that they can be costly and the quality of the firms varies. Make sure you understand the fee structure and what they will do for you before you sign anything.

3. Temporary employment firms

Temporary employment firms offer a variety of employment services to both applicants and employers who are either looking for temporary work and workers or who want to better screen applicants and employers. Many of these firms, such as Manpower (www.man power.com), Olsten (olsten.com), and Kelly Services (kellyservices. com), recruit individuals for a wide range of positions and skill levels as well as full-time employment. Some firms specialize in certain types of workers, such as IT and computer personnel. If you are interested in "testing the job waters," you may want to contact these firms. Employers pay for these services. While most firms are listed in the community Yellow Pages, many also operate websites. The following websites are especially popular with individuals interested in part-time, temporary, or contract work: net-temps.com, www.rhii. com, eLance.com, ework.com, emoonlighter.com, aquent.com, dice. com, parttimejobstore.com, talentmarket.monster.com, and talent gateway.com.

4. College/university placement offices

College and university placement offices provide in-house career planning services for graduating students. While some assist alumni, don't expect too much help if you have already graduated; contact the alumni office which may offer employment services. Many college placement offices are understaffed or provide only rudimen-

tary services, such as maintaining a career planning library, coordi-
nating on-campus interviews for graduating seniors, and conducting
workshops on how to write resumes and handle interviews. Others
provide a full range of well supported services including testing and
one-on-one counseling. Many community colleges also offer such
services to members of the community on a walk-in basis. You can
use their libraries and computerized career assessment programs,
take personality and interest inventories, or attend special workshops or full-semester career planning courses which will take you
through each step of the career planning and job search processes.
Check with your local campus to see what services you might use.
Many of the college and university placement offices belong to the
National Association of Colleges and Employers (NACE), which
operates its own employment website: www.jobweb.com. This site
includes a wealth of information on employment for college
graduates. Its "Catapult" section provides direct links to hundreds
of college and university placement offices: www.jobweb.com/cata
pult. To find college alumni offices, visit the following websites:
alumni.net and www.bcharrispub.com,

5. Private career and job search firms

Private career and job search firms help individuals acquire job
search skills and coach them through the process of finding a job.
They do not find you a job. Expect to pay anywhere from $1,500 to
$10,000 for this service. If you need a structured environment for
conducting your job search, contact these firms for assistance. One
of the oldest such firms is Bernard Haldane Associates, which is now
known as BH Careers International. Since the 1990s, this firm has
had a troubled history, including many lawsuits from unhappy
clients who have charged it with fraud and deceptive practices.
Nonetheless, this company has been a pioneer in the field of career
planning and management. Many of its career planning and job
search methods are incorporated in this book as well as can be found
in five other key job search books: *Haldane's Best Resumes for
Professionals, Haldane's Best Cover Letters for Professionals,
Haldane's Best Answers to Tough Interview Questions,
Haldane's Best Salary Tips for Professionals*, and *Haldane's
Best Employment Websites for Professionals*. This firm has over

50 branches located in the U.S., Canada, Australia, and the United Kingdom. Other firms offering related services include Right Management Associates (right.com) and R. L. Stevens & Associates (interviewing.com), and Lee Hecht Harrison (lhh.com/us).

6. Executive search firms and headhunters

Executive search firms work for employers in finding employees to fill critical positions in the $50,000 plus salary range. They also are called "headhunters," "management consultants," and "executive recruiters." Don't expect to contract for these services. Executive recruiters work for employers, not applicants. On the other hand, you may want to contact firms that specialize in recruiting individuals with your skill specialty. For a comprehensive listing of these firms, see the latest annual edition of *The Directory of Executive Recruiters* (Kennedy Information, kennedyinfo.com). Several companies we identified in Chapter 7, such as resumezapper. com, blastmyresume.com, and resumeblaster.com, offer email resume blasting services that primarily target executive recruiters. As noted earlier, approach these services with a sense of healthy skepticism.

7. Marketing services

Marketing services represent an interesting combination of job search and executive search activities. They can cost $2,500 or more, and they work with individuals anticipating a starting salary of at least $75,000 but preferably over $100,000. A typical operation begins with a client paying a $150 fee for developing psychological, skills, and interests profiles. A marketing plan is outlined and a contract signed for specific services. The firm normally develops a slick "professional" resume and sends it by mail or e-mail, along with a cover letter, to hundreds – maybe thousands – of firms. Clients are then briefed and sent to interviews. Again, approach these services with caution and with the knowledge that you can probably do just as well – if not better – on your own by following the step-by-step advice of this and other job search books.

8. Women's centers and special career services

Women's centers and special career services for displaced workers, such as 40-Plus Clubs (40plus.org/chapters) and Five O'Clock Clubs (fiveoclockclub.com), have been established to respond to the employment needs of special groups. Women's centers are particularly active in sponsoring career planning workshops and job information networks. Special career services arise at times for different categories of employees. For example, unemployed aerospace engineers, teachers, veterans, air traffic controllers, and government employees have formed special groups for developing job search skills and sharing job leads.

9. Testing and assessment centers

Testing and assessment centers provide assistance for identifying vocational skills, interests, and objectives. Usually staffed by trained professionals, these centers administer several types of tests and charge from $300 to $800 per person. You may wish to use some of these services if you feel our activities in Chapters 2 and 8 generate insufficient information on your skills and interests to formulate your job objective. If you use such services, make sure you are given one or both of the two most popular and reliable tests: *Myers-Briggs Type Indicator®* and the *Strong Interest Inventory®*. You should find both tests helpful in better understanding your interests and decision-making styles. The career office at your local community college or women's center may administer these tests at minimum cost. At the same time, many of these testing and assessment services are now available online. We identified several of these websites at the end of Chapter 8.

10. Job fairs and career conferences

Job fairs and career conferences are organized by a variety of groups – from schools and government agencies to executive recruiters, employment agencies, and professional associations – to link applicants to employers. Held over one to two days in a hotel or conference center, employers give presentations on their companies, applicants circulate resumes, and employers interview candidates.

Many such conferences are organized to attract hard-to-recruit groups, such as engineers, computer programmers, and clerical and service workers. These are excellent sources for job leads and information on specific employers – if you are invited to attend or if the meeting is open to the public. Employers pay for this service, although some job fairs or career conferences may charge job seekers a nominal registration fee.

11. Professional associations

Professional associations often provide placement assistance. This usually consists of listing job vacancies in publications, maintaining a resume database, and organizing a job information exchange at annual conferences. Many large associations operate their own online employment sites; members can include their resume in an electronic database and employers can access the database to search for qualified candidates. Annual conferences are good sources for making job contacts in different geographic locations within a particular professional field. But don't expect too much. Talking to people (networking) at professional conferences may yield better results than reading job listings, placing your resume in a database, or interviewing at conference placement centers. For excellent online directories of professional associations, be sure to visit these sites: ipl.org/div/aon and www.asaenet.org.

12. Professional resume writers

Professional resume writers play an important role in career planning. Each year thousands of job seekers rely on these professionals for assistance in writing their resumes. Many of them also provide useful job search tips on resume distribution, cover letters, and networking. Charging from $100 to $500 for writing a resume, they work with the whole spectrum of job seekers – entry-level to senior executives making millions of dollars each year. While not certified career counselors, many of these professionals have their own associations and certification groups. If you are interested in using a professional resume writer, visit these websites for information on this network of career professionals: www.parw.com, prwra.com, and nrwaweb.com. Also, review our recommendations in Chapter 9.

Locating a Certified Career Professional

Certified career professionals have their own associations. If you are interested in contacting one for assistance, we advise you to first visit these websites for locating a career professional:

- National Board for Certified
  Counselors, Inc.   nbcc.org
- National Career
  Development Association   ncda.org
- Certified Career Coaches   certifiedcareercoaches.com
- Career Planning and Adult
  Development Network   careernetwork.org

Dealing With Difficult Backgrounds

If, as we noted in Chapter 1, you have a difficult or not-so-hot background that requires special intervention – from counseling to therapy – by all means seek professional assistance. You are one of the more neglected groups when it comes to employment assistance. While the tips and strategies outlined in this book should prove very useful, you may need additional assistance that goes beyond the scope of this book. Individuals with backgrounds involving incarceration, drug and alcohol abuse, mental illness, and learning disabilities may find assistance through local social service departments, Workforce Development Programs, hospitals, YMCAs, YWCAs, churches, and other local nonprofit groups (Goodwill Industries, Project RIO, Welcome Home Ministries) experienced in working with such individuals. We also publish a unique catalog of nearly 300 career-related resources relevant to individuals with difficult but promising backgrounds. You can download a copy of this catalog at:

www.impactpublications.com

We also maintain a separate website for ex-offenders:

www.exoffenderreentry.com

The catalog and website should prove useful in dealing with many special career-related problems of people with difficult backgrounds.

18

Resist Changing Behaviors and Acquiring New Habits of Success

I F YOU HAVE A PATTERN OF behavior that works against your best career interests, it's time to face reality and do something about it. We know people can change their behaviors and acquire new habits of success, but only if they recognize and accept the need to change, become motivated, and then make a concerted effort to bring about the necessary changes. In other words, they **take action**.

We're not talking about just understanding your patterns and engaging in wishful thinking about the future. We're talking about taking action that has long-term consequences for changing your life for the better.

Minor and Major Behavioral Changes

No one was born with bad habits. Since most have been learned over time, they also can be unlearned and changed – hopefully in less time!

Many changes you may need to make in your behavior are relatively minor and easy to make. In fact, you can probably avoid 90 percent of the mistakes outlined in this book because you are now knowledgeable about the need to change how you conduct your job search. For example, knowing that you should never talk about salary before receiving a job offer or the importance of writing a nice thank-you letter after an interview, may be new behaviors but behaviors you can easily acquire given a combination of knowledge and tips on how you can better make the job search process work to your advantage.

However, other behaviors, especially recurring habits, are more difficult to change and require more work on your part. For example, if you have a bad habit of using poor grammar and vocalized pauses when speaking with others, or if you make lots of spelling and punctuation errors when you write, you'll have to work hard at breaking those habits.

No one was born with bad habits. Since most have been learned over time, they also can be unlearned and changed – hopefully in less time!

They most likely are patterns you have acquired over the years. If you can't break those habits, they will be held against you in the job market as well as on the job. Employers don't want to hire or advance people who communicate poorly and thus reflect badly on their organization. You may need to go back to school to take courses or hire a professional to help you improve your writing and speaking skills. If you have been making these errors most of your life, it's time you did something about changing such bad habits. They can be broken and corrected. These are learning problems that can be corrected if you are sufficiently motivated to find the time and make the effort to change your behavior.

The same is true for other bad habits that will be held against you in the workplace – being inaccurate, irresponsible, late, procrastinating, rude, disrespectful, unfocused, lazy, dishonest, or arrogant. These may be more difficult behavioral patterns to change, but they can be changed nonetheless. But you first need to admit you have a problem and then commit yourself to making the necessary changes. But you must go beyond understanding, acceptance, and commitment. You must be sufficiently motivated to change your life by taking specific actions to change behavior. In many respects, the process of admitting you have a problem and then committing yourself to making the necessary changes is no different from breaking any addictive behavior, be it overeating, alcohol and drug abuse, smoking, or excessive use of television and the Internet.

A Gallery of Career-Limiting Behaviors

Employers know all too well that many workplace behaviors are difficult to change. Many people develop bad habits or workplace sins that get them into trouble. Several such behaviors can get you fired or ostracized from work groups. They are easily recognizable by employers who must evaluate employees and by co-workers you interact with. Do you suspect any of the following negative workplace behaviors describe you in the eyes of your employers and co-workers? Circle the ones that might pertain to you.

- uncooperative
- untrustworthy
- insincere
- negative
- domineering
- disrespectful
- irresponsible
- lack initiative
- impatient
- disruptive
- loud
- boring
- stupid
- selfish
- inaccurate
- unhappy
- deceitful
- unreliable
- extravagant
- inattentive
- dangerous
- hot-tempered
- depressed
- manic
- superficial
- uninterested
- weird
- talkative
- incompetent
- vicious
- forgetful
- unprepared
- overwhelmed

- arrogant
- self-centered
- tactless
- disorganized
- unfocused
- snippy
- rude
- unpredictable
- resistant
- late
- unproductive
- dishonest
- disingenuous
- destructive
- error-prone
- odd
- incoherent
- unsteady
- wasteful
- unstable
- stressed
- uncontrollable
- confused
- slow
- lazy
- spacey
- desperate
- oppressive
- borderline
- unforgiving
- procrastinating
- illiterate
- phony

- lethargic
- ignorant
- problematic
- careless
- unrelenting
- insubordinate

- disloyal
- addicted
- sloppy
- disagreeable
- crazy

While some of these behaviors occur once or twice with people, they often are noticeable patterns of behavior. Many are difficult to change without professional help. For example, being late and slow can be corrected by paying attention to the clock and setting production goals within specific time frames. But negative attitudes, insincerity, depression, rudeness, inaccuracy, impatience, and dishonesty may require some combination of attitude adjustment, coaching, training, and therapy to change such negative behaviors.

Change Your Attitudes

Many changes in behavior first require changes in attitudes. Begin by opening your mind to a new world of possibilities. Start by listening carefully to your inner voice – what does it say to you about others? Is it usually positive and supportive of others or is it often negative and self-centered? If, for example, you tend to be rude to others, it's important to examine your attitudes toward others. Why, for example, do you treat others rudely? Is that how you want other people to treat you? Remember, what goes around often comes around. Positive and enthusiastic people tend to attract people with similar attitudes toward others and their work. Employers want to hire people who focus on getting their work done in cooperation with others. It's imperative that you have good communication and social skills that are clearly reflected in your attitude, which should be positive and proactive. If you want to change your attitudes, review our recommended resources in Chapter 3.

Acquire New Habits for Success

A habit is something you have learned and routinized to the point where you don't need to think about doing it. Since habits are learned, they can be changed by acknowledging them and developing new routines that replace the old habits. You need to reprogram your brain to develop these new replacement habits. Start doing this by completing the following exercise for changing at least five habits. In the first column, acknowledge habits that might be career-limiting. These might include procrastination, lack of initiative, smoking, getting stressed, impatience, and fear of speaking before a group. In the second column, identify what new habits you would like to replace each career-limiting habit with:

Career-Limiting Habits (Habits to Eliminate)	**Career-Enhancing Habits** (New Habits to Acquire)
1. _____	_____
2. _____	_____
3. _____	_____
4. _____	_____
5. _____	_____

Develop a four-week plan to change each of your career-limiting habits. Write down exactly what actions you will take each day to acquire your new habit of success. If, for example, procrastination is one of your career-limiting habits, immediately read Brian Tracy's *Eat That Frog!* and start practicing his 21 ways to stop procrastination. You'll be amazed how quickly – within 24 hours – you can change your procrastinating behavior to that of taking greater initiative in getting things done in a timely and efficient manner. Within a couple of weeks of practicing the new behaviors, your past habit of procrastination should disappear as you make a habit of getting things done. If you approach each of our other career-limiting habits in a similar manner, they too should soon disappear and be replaced with career-enhancing habits.

Useful Habit-Changing Resources

Several of the following books should help change your career-limiting habits in the direction of career-enhancing habits:

The 7 Habits of Highly Effective People
17 Lies That Are Holding Your Back and the Truth That Will
   Set You Free
100 Ways to Motivate Yourself
The Addiction Workbook
Change Your Attitude
Denial Is Not a River in Egypt
Eat That Frog!
Failing Forward
Focal Point
Forgiveness
Habit Busting
The Habit Change Workbook
If Life Is a Game, These Are the Rules
If Success Is a Game, These Are the Rules
Maximum Success
One Day My Soul Just Opened Up
Passages Through Recovery
The Power of Purpose
Reinventing Yourself
Sex, Drugs, Gambling and Chocolate
Self Matters
Stop the Chaos
The Truth About Addiction and Recovery
Understanding the Twelve Steps
Who Moved My Cheese?
You Can Heal Your Life

Many People Want to Hire You!

If you closely examine the 17 mistakes job seekers make (Chapters 2-18) and commit yourself to changing your behaviors and replacing career-limiting habits with new career-enhancing habits, you'll discover a whole new world of employers and organizations that recognize your skills and abilities. You should get interviews and job offers because you conducted a positive, proactive, and employer-centered job search that emphasized your patterns of performance. All you need is to convince yourself to **do it now!**

19

What's Your Behavioral Advantage?

WHAT DIFFERENTIATES YOU from other candidates in today's job market? What makes you so special in comparison to other job seekers and employees? Is it your education, skills, experience, personality, attitude, or level of performance? Do you have certain defining characteristics that clearly communicate your future value to employers and set you apart from others?

Employers Focus on Total Behavior

While employers want to know if **you can do the job**, they are more interested in learning if **you can work with them**. They want to know if there will be good chemistry between you and other employees. It's that chemistry which contributes to the success of their operations and differentiates them from other organizations or companies.

If you want to avoid the 17 mistakes outlined in previous chapters, you are well advised to identify and communicate your behavioral advantage to employers. Learn what makes you so unique and how that uniqueness fits into a company and contributes to its success. Discover what differentiates you behaviorally in the workplace. What makes you likable to employers? While you may impress employers with your resume, letters, interview answers, and stories of past accomplishments, it's your **total behavior** that really distinguishes you from other candidates. Employers "read between the lines" for behavioral clues when they examine resumes and letters, interview candidates, or do background checks and testing. How well you may do the job is only one of their many behavioral concerns. They also want to know how well you work with co-workers, managers, and clients; whether you just meet expectations or constantly exceed expectations; to what extent you bring out the best in others and attract success; and how well you contribute to the overall success of the company or organization.

You Are Unique and Special

Everyone is unique when it comes to their behavior. They have special qualities that can contribute to the success of employers' operations. Your job is to make sure you understand what makes you unique and special and then communicate that uniqueness to potential employers. Starting with setting goals in Chapter 2, identifying accomplishments in Chapter 7, and developing an attractive pattern of work behavior in Chapter 11, you should now have an important story to tell employers about how your total behavior relates to their hiring needs. If you can do that, you will never utter the often heard lament of the frustrated job seeker, *"No one will hire me!"* Instead, employers will readily seek you out and say *"We're interested in hiring you,"* because you have a distinct behavioral advantage they both need and want for their operations.

Index

The Authors

FOR MORE THAN TWO DECADES Ron and Caryl Krannich have pursued a passion – assisting hundreds of thousands of individuals, from students, the unemployed, and ex-offenders to military personnel, international job seekers, and CEOs, in making critical job and career transitions. Focusing on key job search skills, career changes, and employment fields, their impressive body of work has helped shape career thinking and behavior both in the United States and abroad. Their sound advice has changed numerous lives, including their own!

Ron and Caryl are two of America's leading career and travel writers who have authored more than 80 books. A former Peace Corps Volunteer and Fulbright Scholar, Ron received his Ph.D. in Political Science from Northern Illinois University. Caryl received her Ph.D. in Speech Communication from Penn State University. Together they operate Development Concepts Incorporated, a training, consulting, and publishing firm in Virginia.

The Krannichs are both former university professors, high school teachers, management trainers, and consultants. As trainers and consultants, they have completed numerous projects on management, career development, local government, population planning, and rural development in the United States and abroad. Their career books focus on key job search skills, military and civilian career transitions, government and international careers, travel jobs, and nonprofit organizations and include such classics as *High Impact Resumes and Letters, Interview for Success*, and *Change Your Job, Change Your Life*.

Their books represent one of today's most comprehensive collections of career writing. With over 3 million copies in print, their publications are widely available in bookstores, libraries, and career centers. No strangers to the world of Internet employment and travel, they have written *America's Top Internet Job Sites, Haldane's Best Employment Websites for Professionals, The Directory of Websites for International Jobs*, and *Travel Planning on the Internet* and published several Internet recruitment and job search books. Ron served as the first Work Abroad Advisor to Monster.com. Ron and Caryl also have developed several career-related websites: www.impactpublications.com, www.winningthejob.com, www.exoffenderreentry.com, and www.veterans world.com. Many of their career tips appear on such major websites as www.monster.com, www.careerbuilder.com, www.campuscareercenter. com, and www.employmentguide.com.

Ron and Caryl live a double life with travel being their best kept *"do what you love"* career secret. Authors of more than 20 travel-shopping guidebooks on various destinations around the world, they continue to pursue their international and travel interests through their innovative *Treasures and Pleasures of . . . Best of the Best* travel-shopping series and related websites: www.ishoparoundtheworld.com and www.travel-smarter.com. When not found at their home and business in Virginia, they are probably somewhere in Europe, Asia, Africa, the Middle East, the South Pacific, the Caribbean, or the Americas following their other passion – researching and writing about quality antiques, arts, crafts, jewelry, hotels, restaurants, and sightseeing as well as adhering to the career advice they give to others: *"Pursue a passion that enables you to do what you really love to do."* Their passion is best represented on www.ishoparound theworld.com.

As both career and travel experts, the Krannichs' work is frequently featured in major newspapers, magazines, and newsletters as well as on radio, television, and the Internet. Available for interviews, consultation, and presentations, they can be contacted as follows:

Ron and Caryl Krannich

krannich@impactpublications.com

Career Resources

THE FOLLOWING CAREER RESOURCES are available directly from Impact Publications. Full descriptions of each title as well as downloadable catalogs, videos, software, games, posters, and related products can be found on our website: www.impact publications.com. Complete this form or list the titles, include shipping (see formula at the end), enclose payment, and send your order to:

IMPACT PUBLICATIONS
9104 Manassas Drive, Suite N
Manassas Park, VA 20111-5211 USA
1-800-361-1055 (orders only)
Tel. 703-361-7300 or Fax 703-335-9486
Email address: query@impactpublications.com
Quick & easy online ordering: www.impactpublications.com

Orders from individuals must be prepaid by check, money order, or major credit card. We accept telephone, fax, and email orders.

Qty.	TITLES	Price	TOTAL
Featured Title			
____	No One Will Hire Me!	$15.95	_____
Changing Addictive and Not-So-Hot Behaviors			
____	The Addictive Personality	14.95	_____
____	Angry Men	14.95	_____
____	Angry Women	14.95	_____
____	Denial Is Not a River in Egypt	12.95	_____
____	How to Quit Drugs for Good!	16.95	_____
____	No One Is Unemployable	29.95	_____
____	Passages Through Recovery	14.95	_____
____	Sex, Drugs, Gambling and Chocolate	15.95	_____

_____ Stop the Chaos	12.95	_____
_____ The Truth About Addiction and Recovery	14.00	_____
_____ Understanding the Twelve Steps	12.00	_____
_____ You Can Heal Your Life	12.95	_____

Attitude and Motivation

_____ 100 Ways to Motivate Yourself	14.99	_____
_____ Attitude Is Everything	14.95	_____
_____ Change Your Attitude	15.99	_____
_____ Change Your Thinking, Change Your Life	16.95	_____
_____ Eat That Frog!	13.95	_____
_____ Goals!	15.95	_____
_____ Little Gold Book of YES! Attitude	19.99	_____
_____ Reinventing Yourself	18.99	_____
_____ Success Principles	24.95	_____

Inspiration and Empowerment

_____ 101 Secrets of Highly Effective Speakers	15.95	_____
_____ Create Your Own Future	16.95	_____
_____ The Habit Change Workbook	19.95	_____
_____ Life Strategies	13.95	_____
_____ The Magic of Thinking Big	14.00	_____
_____ The Power of Positive Thinking	12.95	_____
_____ Power of Purpose	20.00	_____
_____ Self Matters	14.00	_____
_____ Seven Habits of Highly Effective People	15.00	_____
_____ The Story of You	19.99	_____
_____ Who Moved My Cheese?	19.95	_____

Testing and Assessment

_____ Career Tests	12.95	_____
_____ Discover What You're Best At	14.00	_____
_____ Do What You Are	18.95	_____
_____ Finding Your Perfect Work	16.95	_____
_____ I Could Do Anything If Only I Knew What It Was	13.95	
_____ I Want to Do Something Else, But I'm Not Sure What It Is	15.95	_____
_____ Now, Discover Your Strengths	30.00	_____
_____ Pathfinder	16.00	_____
_____ Smarts	21.95	_____
_____ What Should I Do With My Life?	14.95	_____
_____ What Type Am I?	14.95	_____
_____ What's Your Type of Career?	18.95	_____
_____ Who Do You Think You Are?	18.00	_____

Career Exploration and Job Strategies

_____ 25 Jobs That Have It All	12.95	_____
_____ 40 Best Fields for Your Career	16.95	_____
_____ 50 Best Jobs for Your Personality	16.95	_____
_____ 50 Cutting Edge Jobs	15.95	_____
_____ 95 Mistakes Job Seekers Make and How to Avoid Them	13.95	_____

_____	100 Great Jobs and How to Get Them	17.95 _____
_____	101 Ways to Recession-Proof Your Career	14.95 _____
_____	225 Best Jobs for Baby Boomers	16.95 _____
_____	250 Best Jobs Through Apprenticeships	24.95 _____
_____	300 Best Jobs Without a Four-Year Degree	16.95 _____
_____	America's Top 100 Jobs for People Without a Four-Year Degree	19.95 _____
_____	America's Top Jobs for People Re-Entering the Workforce	19.95 _____
_____	Best Entry-Level Jobs 2007	16.95 _____
_____	Best Jobs for the 21st Century	19.95 _____
_____	But What If I Don't Want to Go to College?	16.95 _____
_____	Career Change	14.95 _____
_____	Change Your Job, Change Your Life	21.95 _____
_____	Cool Careers for Dummies	19.99 _____
_____	Directory of Executive Recruiters	59.95 _____
_____	Five Secrets to Finding a Job	12.95 _____
_____	How to Get a Job and Keep It	16.95 _____
_____	How to Succeed Without a Career Path	13.95 _____
_____	Job Hunting Guide: From College to Career	14.95 _____
_____	Job Hunting Tips for People With Hot and Not-So-Hot Backgrounds	17.95 _____
_____	Knock 'Em Dead	14.95 _____
_____	Me, Myself, and I, Inc.	17.95 _____
_____	Occupational Outlook Handbook	17.95 _____
_____	O*NET Dictionary of Occupational Titles	39.95 _____
_____	Quit Your Job and Grow Some Hair	15.95 _____
_____	Rites of Passage at $100,000 to $1 Million+	29.95 _____
_____	Top 300 Careers	18.95 _____
_____	What Color Is Your Parachute?	17.95 _____
_____	Your Dream Career for Dummies	16.99 _____

Internet Job Search

_____	100 Top Internet Job Sites	12.95 _____
_____	America's Top Internet Job Sites	19.95 _____
_____	Best Career and Education Websites	12.95 _____
_____	Career Exploration On the Internet	24.95 _____
_____	Directory of Websites for International Jobs	19.95 _____
_____	e-Resumes	16.95 _____
_____	Guide to Internet Job Searching	15.95 _____
_____	Haldane's Best Employment Websites for Professionals	15.95 _____
_____	Job Seeker's Online Goldmine	13.95 _____

Resumes and Letters

_____	101 Great Tips for a Dynamite Resume	13.95 _____
_____	Adams Cover Letter Almanac	17.95 _____
_____	Adams Resume Almanac	17.95 _____
_____	Resume Shortcuts	14.95 _____
_____	Best KeyWords for Resumes, Cover Letters, & Interviews	17.95 _____
_____	Best Resumes and CVs for International Jobs	24.95 _____
_____	Best Resumes for $100,000+ Jobs	24.95 _____
_____	Best Resumes for People Without a Four-Year Degree	19.95 _____
_____	Best Cover Letters for $100,000+ Jobs	24.95 _____
_____	Bioblogs	16.95 _____

____ Blue Collar Resume and Job Hunting Guide	15.95	____
____ Competency-Based Resumes	13.99	____
____ Cover Letter Magic	16.95	____
____ Cover Letters for Dummies	16.99	____
____ Cover Letters That Knock 'Em Dead	12.95	____
____ Create Your Digital Portfolio	19.95	____
____ Expert Resumes for Baby Boomers	16.95	____
____ Expert Resumes for Career Changers	16.95	____
____ Expert Resumes for Computer and Web Jobs	16.95	____
____ Expert Resumes for Managers and Executives	16.95	____
____ Expert Resumes for People Returning to Work	16.95	____
____ Gallery of Best Cover Letters	18.95	____
____ Gallery of Best Resumes	18.95	____
____ Haldane's Best Cover Letters for Professionals	15.95	____
____ Haldane's Best Resumes for Professionals	15.95	____
____ High Impact Resumes and Letters	19.95	____
____ Internet Resumes	14.95	____
____ Military Resumes and Cover Letters	21.95	____
____ Nail the Cover Letter!	17.95	____
____ Nail the Resume!	17.95	____
____ Resume, Application, and Letter Tips for People With Hot and Not-So-Hot Backgrounds	17.95	____
____ Resume Shortcuts	14.95	____
____ Resumes for Dummies	16.99	____
____ Resumes That Knock 'Em Dead	12.95	____
____ The Savvy Resume Writer	12.95	____
____ Step-By-Step Resumes	19.95	____
____ Winning Letters That Overcome Barriers to Employment	17.95	____
____ World's Greatest Resumes	14.95	____

Networking

____ Dynamite Telesearch	12.95	____
____ Endless Referrals	16.95	____
____ Fine Art of Small Talk	16.95	____
____ Golden Rule of Schmoozing	12.95	____
____ Great Connections	11.95	____
____ How to Work a Room	14.00	____
____ Little Black Book of Connections	19.95	____
____ Masters of Networking	16.95	____
____ Never Eat Alone	24.95	____
____ One Phone Call Away	24.95	____
____ Power Networking	14.95	____
____ The Savvy Networker	13.95	____
____ Shortcut Your Job Search	12.95	____
____ Work the Pond!	15.95	____

Dress, Image, and Etiquette

____ Dressing Smart for Men	16.95	____
____ Dressing Smart for the New Millennium	15.95	____
____ Dressing Smart for Women	16.95	____
____ New Professional Image	14.95	____
____ Power Etiquette	15.95	____
____ You've Only Got Three Seconds	15.00	____

Interviews

_____	101 Dynamite Questions to Ask At Your Job Interview	13.95 _____
_____	301 Smart Answers to Tough Interview Questions	10.95 _____
_____	Adams Job Interview Almanac	17.95 _____
_____	Don't Blow the Interview	12.95 _____
_____	Haldane's Best Answers to Tough Interview Questions	15.95 _____
_____	I Can't Believe They Asked Me That!	17.95 _____
_____	Interview for Success	15.95 _____
_____	Interview Magic	16.95 _____
_____	Job Interview Tips for People With Not-So-Hot Backgrounds	14.95 _____
_____	Job Interviews for Dummies	16.99 _____
_____	KeyWords to Nail Your Job Interview	17.95 _____
_____	Mastering the Job Interview	19.95 _____
_____	Nail the Job Interview!	13.95 _____
_____	The Savvy Interviewer	10.95 _____
_____	Sweaty Palms	13.95 _____
_____	Tell Your Story, Win the Job	19.95 _____
_____	Winning the Interview Game	12.95 _____

Salary Negotiations

_____	Dynamite Salary Negotiations	15.95 _____
_____	Get a Raise in 7 Days	14.95 _____
_____	Negotiating Your Salary	12.95 _____
_____	Salary Negotiation Tips for Professionals	16.95 _____
_____	Secrets of Power Salary Negotiating	13.99 _____

Military in Transition

_____	Expert Resumes for Military-to-Civilian Transition	16.95 _____
_____	Jobs and the Military Spouse	17.95 _____
_____	Military Resumes and Cover Letters	21.95 _____
_____	Military-to-Civilian Career Transition Guide	15.95 _____
_____	Military to Federal Career Guide	38.95 _____
_____	Military Transition to Civilian Success	21.95 _____

Ex-Offenders in Transition

_____	9 to 5 Beats Ten to Life	15.00 _____
_____	99 Days and a Get Up	9.95 _____
_____	Best Resumes and Letters for Ex-Offenders	19.95 _____
_____	Ex-Offender's Job Hunting Guide	17.95 _____
_____	Ex-Offender's Quick Job Hunting Guide	9.95 _____
_____	Man, I Need a Job	7.95 _____

Government and Security Jobs

_____	Book of U.S. Government Jobs	21.95 _____
_____	Complete Guide to Public Employment	19.95 _____
_____	Federal Applications That Get Results	23.95 _____
_____	FBI Career Guide	15.00 _____
_____	FBI Careers	19.95 _____
_____	Federal Law Enforcement Careers	19.95 _____

_____ Post Office Jobs   19.95 _____
_____ Ten Steps to a Federal Job   39.95 _____

International and Travel Jobs

_____ Back Door Guide to Short-Term Job Adventures   21.95 _____
_____ Big Guide to Living and Working Overseas   49.95 _____
_____ Careers in International Affairs   24.95 _____
_____ The Global Citizen   16.95 _____
_____ Going Global Career Guide   195.95 _____
_____ How to Get a Job in Europe   21.95 _____
_____ International Jobs   19.00 _____
_____ International Job Finder   19.95 _____
_____ Jobs for Travel Lovers   19.95 _____
_____ Teaching English Abroad   19.95 _____
_____ Work Worldwide   14.95 _____
_____ Work Your Way Around the World   19.95 _____

SUBTOTAL   _____

Virginia residents add 5% sales tax   _____

POSTAGE/HANDLING ($5 for first
product and 8% of SUBTOTAL) $5.00

8% of SUBTOTAL --------------------------------------   _____

TOTAL ENCLOSED ------------------------   _____

SHIP TO:

NAME _____

ADDRESS _____

_____

_____

PAYMENT METHOD:

❑ I enclose check/money order for $ _____ made payable to
   IMPACT PUBLICATIONS.

❑ Please charge $ _____ to my credit card:
   ❑ Visa   ❑ MasterCard   ❑ American Express   ❑ Discover

   Card # _____ Expiration date: ____/____

   Signature _____

The Career Savvy Series

Resume, Application, and Letter Tips for People with Hot and Not-So-Hot Backgrounds
185 Tips for Landing the Perfect Job
Ron and Caryl Krannich, Ph.Ds

Each year over 25 million Americans conduct a job search that involves writing resumes and letters and/or completing applications. However, many of these job seekers make numerous writing mistakes that prevent them from landing job interviews. Reflecting the experiences of many job seekers, employers, and career experts, this book outlines 185 tips for creating more effective resumes, letters, and applications. Rich with quizzes, examples, and websites. ISBN 1-57023-240-7. 2006. 224 pages. $17.95

Job Hunting Tips for People With Hot and Not-So-Hot Backgrounds
150 Smart Tips That Can Change Your Life
Ron and Caryl Krannich, Ph.Ds

Finding a job may be the hardest, most frustrating, and ego-bruising work you will ever do. Depending on how you approach the process, it can also be an extremely educational, exciting, and exhilarating experience. This unique book presents 150 job hunting tips that are applicable to most job seekers, regardless of their backgrounds. Organized around a step-by-step job search process, it includes tips on everything from conducting a self-assessment, developing an objective, and conducting research to completing applications, writing resumes and letters, networking, interviewing, and negotiating salary. 2005. 240 pages. ISBN 1-57023-225-3. $17.95

Job Interview Tips for People With Not-So-Hot Backgrounds
Ron and Caryl Krannich, Ph.Ds.

You must do well in the job interview to get a job offer. But what should you say and do if your background includes red flags – you've been incarcerated, got fired, received poor grades, or lack necessary skills? This book speaks to millions of individuals who have difficult but promising backgrounds. Shows how to best prepare for interview questions that could become job knock-outs. Filled with numerous examples and cases to illustrate how to provide honest and positive answers. 2004. ISBN 1-57023-213-X. $14.95

Also available in series at www.impactpublications.com:

- 95 Mistakes Job Seekers Make ($13.95)
- No One Will Hire Me! ($15.95)
- Savvy Interviewing ($10.95)
- The Savvy Networker ($13.95)
- The Savvy Resume Writer ($12.95)

Keep in Touch...
On the Web!

www.impactpublications.com
www.ishoparoundtheworld.com
www.exoffenderreentry.com
www.travel-smarter.com
www.winningthejob.com
www.veteransworld.com